# First World War
## and Army of Occupation
# War Diary
## France, Belgium and Germany

21 DIVISION
Divisional Troops
96 Brigade Royal Field Artillery
10 September 1915 - 27 December 1916

WO95/2143/1

The Naval & Military Press Ltd
www.nmarchive.com
**Published in association with The National Archives**

Published by

## The Naval & Military Press Ltd

Unit 10 Ridgewood Industrial Park,

Uckfield, East Sussex,

TN22 5QE England

Tel: +44 (0) 1825 749494

www.naval-military-press.com

www.nmarchive.com

*This diary has been reprinted in facsimile from the original. Any imperfections are inevitably reproduced and the quality may fall short of modern type and cartographic standards.*

© **Crown Copyright**
**Images reproduced by permission of The National Archives, London, England, 2015.**

# Contents

| Document type | Place/Title | Date From | Date To |
|---|---|---|---|
| Heading | 2143/1 96 Brigade Royal Artillery | | |
| Heading | 21st Division 96th Bde R.F.A. Sep 1915-Dec 1916 Broken Up | | |
| Heading | War Diary Headquarters 96th Brigade R.F.A. (21st Division) September (10.9.15 To 30.9.15) 1915 | | |
| War Diary | Milford | 10/09/1915 | 10/09/1915 |
| War Diary | Southampton | 10/09/1915 | 10/09/1915 |
| War Diary | Havre | 11/09/1915 | 12/09/1915 |
| War Diary | St. Omer | 13/09/1915 | 13/09/1915 |
| War Diary | Tournehem | 13/09/1915 | 15/09/1915 |
| War Diary | Staples | 16/09/1915 | 16/09/1915 |
| War Diary | St Jans Cappel | 16/09/1915 | 21/09/1915 |
| War Diary | ? Miquellerie | 21/09/1915 | 22/09/1915 |
| War Diary | Bas Rieux | 22/09/1915 | 24/09/1915 |
| War Diary | Haillicourt | 24/09/1915 | 25/09/1915 |
| War Diary | Noeux Les Mines | 25/09/1915 | 25/09/1915 |
| War Diary | Noeux Les Mines | 25/09/1915 | 26/09/1915 |
| War Diary | Fosse No 7 de Bethune | 27/09/1915 | 30/09/1915 |
| Heading | 21st Division 96th Bde R.F.A. Vol 2 Oct 15 | | |
| War Diary | Fosse No 7 de Bethune | 01/10/1915 | 02/10/1915 |
| War Diary | Mazingarbe | 03/10/1915 | 03/10/1915 |
| War Diary | Mazingarbe Meuxles Mines | 03/10/1915 | 04/10/1915 |
| War Diary | Merville | 04/10/1915 | 05/10/1915 |
| War Diary | Hazebrouck | 05/10/1915 | 08/10/1915 |
| War Diary | Armentieres | 09/10/1915 | 31/10/1915 |
| Heading | 21st Division 96th Bde Div. R.F.A. Vol 3 Nov 15 | | |
| War Diary | Armentieres | 01/11/1915 | 30/11/1915 |
| Heading | 21st Division 96th Bde R.F.A. Vol 4 | | |
| War Diary | Armentieres | 01/12/1915 | 31/12/1915 |
| Operation(al) Order(s) | 96th Bde Operation Order No.2 | | |
| Miscellaneous | Table A | | |
| Miscellaneous | Table B | | |
| Miscellaneous | | 14/12/1915 | 14/12/1915 |
| Miscellaneous | A Form Messages And Signals | | |
| Miscellaneous | 96th Brigade RFA | 24/12/1915 | 24/12/1915 |
| Miscellaneous | BM 31/7 | 16/12/1915 | 16/12/1915 |
| Miscellaneous | Officer Commanding 96th Brigade | 18/12/1915 | 18/12/1915 |
| Miscellaneous | Special Brigade Order By Brigadier General E.R. Hill Commanding 63rd Infantry Brigade. | 16/12/1915 | 16/12/1915 |
| Miscellaneous | C Form (Duplicate) Messages And Signals | | |
| Map | | | |
| Operation(al) Order(s) | 96th Bde Orders (Operation) No. 5 | 26/12/1915 | 26/12/1915 |
| Miscellaneous | Table "A" | | |
| Operation(al) Order(s) | 96 Bde Operation Order No. 6 | 30/12/1915 | 30/12/1915 |
| Miscellaneous | To B/96 C/96 D/96 | 31/12/1915 | 31/12/1915 |
| Heading | 21st Divisional Artillery 96th Brigade R.F.A. January 1916 | | |
| War Diary | Armentieres | 01/01/1916 | 31/01/1916 |
| Operation(al) Order(s) | Operation Order No. 7 | 07/01/1916 | 07/01/1916 |
| Operation(al) Order(s) | 96th Bde Operation Order No. 8 | | |

| | | | |
|---|---|---|---|
| Operation(al) Order(s) | 96th Bde. Operation Order No. 7 | 10/01/1916 | 10/01/1916 |
| Heading | 21st Divisional Artillery 96th Brigade R.F.A. February 1916 | | |
| War Diary | Armentieres | 01/02/1916 | 29/02/1916 |
| Operation(al) Order(s) | 96th Bde Operation Order No. 10 | | |
| Operation(al) Order(s) | 96th Bde Operation Order No. 9 | 10/12/1916 | 10/12/1916 |
| Operation(al) Order(s) | 96th Bde Operation Order No. 11 | 23/02/1916 | 23/02/1916 |
| Miscellaneous | Table "A" | | |
| Miscellaneous | Table "B" Bombardment And Assault | 24/02/1916 | 24/02/1916 |
| Miscellaneous | Table "C" | | |
| Heading | 21st Divisional Artillery 96th Brigade R.F.A. March 1916 | | |
| War Diary | Armentieres | 01/03/1916 | 29/03/1916 |
| War Diary | La Kreule | 30/03/1916 | 31/03/1916 |
| Diagram etc | System of Telephone Communications March 1916 | | |
| Heading | 21st Divisional Artillery 96th Brigade R.F.A. April 1916 | | |
| War Diary | Bussy-Les Daours | 01/04/1916 | 26/04/1916 |
| Heading | 21st Divisional Artillery 96th Brigade R.F.A. May 1916 | | |
| War Diary | Bussy-Les Daours | 01/05/1916 | 04/05/1916 |
| War Diary | Becordel | 05/05/1916 | 31/05/1916 |
| Heading | 21st Divisional Artillery 96th Brigade R.F.A. June 1916 | | |
| War Diary | Becordel | 01/06/1916 | 01/08/1916 |
| Miscellaneous | Instructions For Office No. 4 Barrages | 18/06/1916 | 18/06/1916 |
| Miscellaneous | Table "L" Fricourt Attack Special Zero Time | | |
| Heading | 21st Divisional Artillery 96th Brigade R.F.A. July 1916 | | |
| War Diary | | 02/07/1916 | 10/07/1916 |
| War Diary | Mametz | 11/07/1916 | 16/07/1916 |
| War Diary | Bazentin Le-Petit | 17/07/1916 | 24/07/1916 |
| War Diary | Bonnay | 24/07/1916 | 24/07/1916 |
| Operation(al) Order(s) | 96th Brigade Operation Order No. 1 | 16/06/1916 | 16/06/1916 |
| Miscellaneous | Smoke And Gas Barrages Smoke | 19/06/1916 | 19/06/1916 |
| Miscellaneous | Table "A" Wirecutting "U" Day | | |
| Map | Wire Cut By 96th Bde June 24-30th | | |
| Miscellaneous | Table "B" Period 9.30 pm. "U" to 9.30 p.m. "V" | | |
| Miscellaneous | Table "B" Period 9.30 p.m. "U" to 9.30 p.m. "V" | | |
| Miscellaneous | Table "C" Period 9.30 p.m. V to 9.10 p.m. "W" | | |
| Miscellaneous | Table D Period 9.30 p.m. "W" to 9.30 "X" | | |
| Miscellaneous | Table "E" Period 9.30 pm "X" to 9.30 "Y" | | |
| Miscellaneous | Table "B"-26th Brigade R.F.A. | | |
| Miscellaneous | A6 BM/100/2 | | |
| Miscellaneous | Table "F" Period From 9.30 pm "Y" Day to Zero Time "Z" Day. | | |
| Miscellaneous | Smoke Barrages Table | | |
| Miscellaneous | Table "M" D/96th Bde. R.F.A. 4.5 "Hours" | | |
| Heading | 21st Divisional Artillery 96th Brigade R.F.A. August 1916 | | |
| War Diary | | 24/07/1916 | 31/08/1916 |
| War Diary | | 03/08/1916 | 29/08/1916 |
| Heading | 21st Divisional Artillery 96th Brigade R.F.A. September 1916 | | |
| War Diary | | 01/09/1916 | 01/10/1916 |
| Heading | 21st Divisional Artillery 96th Brigade R.F.A. October 1916 | | |
| War Diary | Somme | 01/10/1916 | 22/10/1916 |
| War Diary | Annequin | 22/10/1916 | 31/10/1916 |

| | | | |
|---|---|---|---|
| Miscellaneous | 21st Divisional Artillery Instructions For Relief No.1 | 12/10/1916 | 12/10/1916 |
| Miscellaneous | B Gun Position O.P.S. A Wagon Lines Of 96th Bde R.F.A. (Cambrin Group) | 31/10/1916 | 31/10/1916 |
| Heading | 21st Divisional Artillery 96th Brigade R.F.A. November 1916 | | |
| War Diary | | 11/11/1916 | 12/11/1916 |
| Heading | 21st Divisional Artillery 96th Brigade R.F.A. December 1916 | | |
| War Diary | Annequin | 07/12/1916 | 11/12/1916 |
| War Diary | Noyelles | 12/12/1916 | 27/12/1916 |

2143/1

96 Brigade Royal Artillery

21ST DIVISION

96TH BDE R.F.A.
SEP 1915-DEC 1916

BROKEN UP

Brigade disembarked
Havre from England
11.9.15.

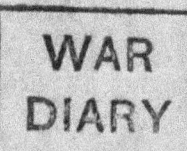

Headquarters,

96th BRIGADE, R.F.A.

(21st Division)

S E P T E M B E R

(10.9.15 to 30.9.15)

1 9 1 5

Sheet 1
Army Form C. 2118.

# WAR DIARY
## or
## INTELLIGENCE SUMMARY.
(Erase heading not required.)

9567 R.F.A.

Instructions regarding War Diaries and Intelligence Summaries are contained in F.S. Regs., Part II. and the Staff Manual respectively. Title pages will be prepared in manuscript.

| Place | Date | Hour | Summary of Events and Information | Remarks and references to Appendices |
|---|---|---|---|---|
| Hatfield | 10/9/15 | 2 a.m. | 91st Bryad R.F.A. left Hatfield. | |
| Southampton | " | 4 p.m. | Arrived at Docks | |
| Havre | 11/9/15 | 10.30 a.m. | Entrained in fact and proceeded to No. 5 Camp Havre | |
| " | 12/9/15 | 2.30 p.m. | Entrained for Aire ourcq | |
| St. Omer | 13/9/15 | 10.40 a.m. | Arrived and left immediately for Hazebrouck | |
| Hazebrouck | " | 4 p.m. | Arrived in billets. | |
| " | 14/9/15 | | At Hazebrouck. | |
| " | 15/9/15 | 6 a.m. | Left for watering and stunts to Staples | |
| " | 16/9/15 | 9 a.m. | Left for St. Jans Cappel. | |
| Staples | | | | |
| St. Jans Cappel | 16/9/15 | 3 p.m. | Arrived. | |
| | 17/9/15 | | Nine officers accompanied by signallers & gunners left for firing line - attached to 12th Div. | |
| | | | at Hasque for experience. | |
| | 18/9/15 | | Gun drill & signalling practice. | |
| | 19/9/15 | | " " | |
| | 20/9/15 | 9 a.m. | The nine officers and signallers returned to Brigade. | |
| | 21/9/15 | 9 a.m. | Left for Hazebrouck where Brigade rejoined remainder of Div. Art. continued marching | |
| | | | via Morville & Ruesnes | |
| a. Mayhenew | 22/9/15 | 3.15 p.m. | After 9.30 arrived. | |
| | 23/9/15 | 9 a.m. | Left for Ros Rieux | |
| Ros Rieux | 23/9/15 | 11.15 a.m. | Arrived | |
| | 23/9/15 | 6 a.m. | 90 rgn. ones issued en route to all guns, also from aeroplane observation | |
| | | | 15 drew 159 rounds H.E. ammunition | |
| | 24/9/15 | 10.30 a.m. | Left for direction of firing line. | |
| Neuvilleux | 24/9/15 | 4.3 a.m. | Arrived and bivouacked. | |
| | | 10 a.m. | Left bivouac | |
| Hamelincourt | | 3 p.m. | Arrived and bivouacked | |

Sheet 2

Army Form 2118

# WAR DIARY
or
# INTELLIGENCE SUMMARY

(Erase heading not required.)

Instructions regarding War Diaries and Intelligence Summaries are contained in F.S. Regs., Part II. and the Staff Manual respectively. Title pages will be prepared in manuscript.

| Place | Date | Hour | Summary of Events and Information | Remarks and references to Appendices |
|---|---|---|---|---|
| Moulin les Vines | 26/8/14 | 8 pm | Left to firing line. Halted for one hour between Mons & de Bettinie, march to a point on Bettinies Rieu Road and took up position for battle in a Ammunition Column about 11:30 p.m. | |
| | 27/8/14 | | Supporting 15th & 2 1st Rio Infantry. 386 rounds fired at various objectives. | |
| | | 6 pm | Positions of Batteries moved slightly forward | |
| Mons le Jo Bettinie | 27/8/14 | 6 am | Batteries and H.Q. all moved up to positions in front of find 15 km South of Jas de Bettinie. Lt Col R.E. Coris temporarily took over Command of 3rd Brigade R.F.A. Major McGowan dispensed took over command of 116 Brigade. 457 rounds fired on 118 Jo. Runfontaine and Halbeau. B Battery heavily shelled for a short time. Casualties O.R. 1 Killed 3 wounded. (Gen Pensenby) Supporting 3rd Cavendi Brigade. | |
| | 28/8/14 | | Canvasting O.R. 1 wounded. Rounds fired 510. | |
| | 29/8/14 | | In action most of day. Casualties O.R. 1 wounded. Rounds fired 36. | |
| | 30/8/14 | | In action most of day. Rounds fired 150. Casualties nil. | |

121/7595

21st Hussars

96th Bde: R.F.A.
Vol 2
Oct 15

Army Form C. 2118.

O/C 4th Brigade RGA  Sheet No. 3

# WAR DIARY
or
# INTELLIGENCE SUMMARY.
(Erase heading not required.)

Instructions regarding War Diaries and Intelligence Summaries are contained in F. S. Regs., Part II. and the Staff Manual respectively. Title pages will be prepared in manuscript.

| Place | Date | Hour | Summary of Events and Information | Remarks and references to Appendices |
|---|---|---|---|---|
| Hotch? du Bahut | 1/10/15 | 7 pm | In action most of day. One section of each battery relieved by one section of 133rd Brigade RGA 13th Division. Casualties O.R. 1 wounded. Rounds fired 50. | |
| | 2·10·15 | | B.C.'s battery heavily shelled. Remaining section of each battery relieved by remaining section of 133rd Brigade RGA. Return line 50. Casualties – 2 Lt. O'Neill, wounded. | |
| | | 8 pm | Our positions and concentrates behind Hog-op-de Bellum. Left for Mazingarbe | |
| | | 10 pm | Brigade arrived outside Mazingarbe village. | |
| | | | During the whole of the above fight the Brigade was under the command of Genl Wardrop. The communication to liaison officer with infantry and also to O.P.'s was extremely difficult owing to lack of wire and to the want of staff. There were continually Lt Col Coull 40, 21st Div out a signal circuit to his operator and were attached for signal 21st Div after stolen operations. It is most essential that a section of Div. signal section for these operations should be always attached to Div. Art. or the Brigades and Battery Company should be able as the units infantry know their own O.P.'s and more than stay can do to look up units infantry know their own O.P.'s all of which lines must be at least duplicated. Runners for communication must be plentiful. | |
| Mazingarbe | 3·10·15 | 8:30 am | Shift for headquarters Menin. | |
| Houchin | 3·10·15 | 9 pm | Arrived at bivouacs. | |
| | 4·10·15 | 3:30 am | Left for Merville | |
| | | 10.3 am | Arrived in billets. | |
| Merville | 5·10·15 | 10 am | Left for Hazebrouck | |

Army Form C. 2118.

## 96th Brigade R.H.A. WAR DIARY

or

## INTELLIGENCE SUMMARY.

Sheet No 4.

(Erase heading not required.)

Instructions regarding War Diaries and Intelligence Summaries are contained in F. S. Regs., Part II and the Staff Manual respectively. Title pages will be prepared in manuscript.

| Place | Date | Hour | Summary of Events and Information | Remarks and references to Appendices |
|---|---|---|---|---|
| Hazebrouck | 5.10.15 | 2.30pm | Arrived in billets. Col Coates returned to command of 96th Bde. Major McKenzie to D/96 to | |
| | 6.10.15 | | at Hazebrouck (in Hondeghem) | |
| | 7.10.15 | 7.45am | Right section of battery left Colonel-Adjutant left for Armentières where they took over positions from Hautturnauer Brigade (50th Division). | |
| | 8.10.15 | 7 am | H.Q. (Rest) & Bde Ammunition Column left for Armentières arriving at 2 pm at La Hippe. H.Q. proceeded to Pont des Nieppes - Signallers going on to Chapelle d'Armentières. | |
| Armentières | 9.10.15 | 7.40 am | Left section of battery left Hazebrouck district for Armentières relieving ur section of 3rd Hautturnauer Brigade (50th Division) | |
| | 9.10.15 | Noon | 96th Bde A.G. 150th & 151st from 3rd North'n Brigade. Reporting in trench HQ & 150th Brigade under General Bush relieved artillerie tactical command of General Stanhope G.O.C. R.A. 50th Division. At this time Col Holiday 10th Div Arty (23rd Division) was on our right. | |
| | 10.10.15 11.10.15 12.10.15 | | Registering on German trenches and retaliation points. Testing and adjusting communications - arranging F.O.O. positions - getting in touch with Infantry Brigades and battalion and trench Commanders. | |
| | 13.10.15 | 2 pm | Wire cutting by D/96 interrupted by Premature discharge of smoke of Infantry trench - light quarters of artillery were most difficult to observe from a distance of about 400 yards. Although general effect seemed good and rifle was received badly broken. A, B & C Batteries co-operated firing on enemy trenches and retaliation points. Very heavy enemy reply. | |
| | 14.10.15 | 2.30pm | Some operation on a minor scale. Enemy reply very weak two stains on predominating. Wagon line have been completing fresh standings for horses and harnessrooms. I should like to record our thanks to the 3rd Northumbrian Brigade for the excellent gun pits they have made and also for the work they have done in the dugouts for house in the way of which stabling for horses were also very telephone communications which they established for us useful. | |

Army Form C. 2118.

# WAR DIARY
## ~~INTELLIGENCE~~ SUMMARY.
*(Erase heading not required.)*

96th Brigade RHA            About No 5.

Instructions regarding War Diaries and Intelligence Summaries are contained in F.S. Regs., Part II. and the Staff Manual respectively. Title pages will be prepared in manuscript.

| Place | Date | Hour | Summary of Events and Information | Remarks and references to Appendices |
|---|---|---|---|---|
| Ammunition | 15.10.15 to 31.10.15 | | Nothing of importance happened beyond daily registration of enemy's possible gun positions which had not been already registered. Wet weather having set in it was found that considerable alteration had to be made to cover of gun pits. Shelled over by 50th D.W. Arty. as there were in almost every case leaking badly. Owing to the break of rain and weight overhead the roofs had sunk in towards the middle thus preventing the water from draining off. | |

96E Mu: D7a.
fol: 3

P/
7678
"

21st Division

Nov 15

Army Form C. 2118

# WAR DIARY
## INTELLIGENCE SUMMARY.

9th Brigade R.F.A.  Sheet No 6

(Erase heading not required.)

Instructions regarding War Diaries and Intelligence Summaries are contained in F. S. Regs., Part II. and the Staff Manual respectively. Title pages will be prepared in manuscript.

| Place | Date | Hour | Summary of Events and Information | Remarks and references to Appendices |
|---|---|---|---|---|
| ARMENTIÈRES | 1/11/15 | | On our right is the 23rd Division and on left 25th Division. Holding the line in front of ARMENTIÈRES. Immediately on right is the 104th Brigade R.F.A commanded by Col. Hole and on left is the 95th Brigade R.F.A commanded by Lt Col Fitzgerald. | |
| | 4.11.15 | | Capt. R.D.M Keatz (O/C C Battery) was returned to U.K. | |
| | 7.11.15 | | Lieut G. Trutt-Dalton was evolved from this Brigade. | |
| | 9.11.15 | 11 a.m. | Lieut G. Trutt-Dalton joined and took over command of C Battery. | |
| | | | B. Battery slightly shelled - one O.R. wounded | |
| | | 3 p.m. | C Battery shelled - three O.R wounded | |
| | | 4 p.m. | D. Battery heavily shelled - one gun slightly damaged | |
| | 11.11.15 and 12.11.15 | | The relief of the 50th Division by 21st Division was completed when its 63rd Iny. Brigade took over trenches by 15/73 from the 150th Iny Bde. The 63rd Iny Bde being commanded by Lt. Col. (Temp Brig) Hill T.F.I. The battalions of this Brigade are 12th West Yorks 8th Lincolns, 8th Yorks & Lancs battns, the 4th battn Middlesex arrival of the Town of ARMENTIÈRES shelled Summarily the Germans were greeting us arrival of the H.Q. 21st Div. receiving special attention. | |
| | | 10.15pm | H.Q of 21st Division | |
| | 14.11.15 | | 15th W Yorks were relieved by a regular battalion i.e. 4th Middlesex Batt | |
| | | 5 p.m. | To commemorate the anniversary of the birth of the Brigade a gathering assembled at the H.Q. mess | |
| | 16.11.15 | 7.30 a.m. | A' staff were arranged for this date but weather being unsuitable it was postponed | |
| | 17.11.15 | | Shoot again postponed on account of weather. Maj Gen Hunter Weston proceeded to 2nd Leah. Brig. Gen G. McCrachy arrived command of Corps artillery. Vice Brig Gen Ja. H.G Nad Artillery adviser 2 Corps. | |
| | 18.11.15 | 7.30 am | Bombardment of Hist Government commenced. The Div Art. 21st Div assisted by the 23rd Div Art. left & all in the heavier co-operated with the aircrafts of circulated aviation. Considerable damage | |

2353 Wt W5344/1454 700,000 5/15 D.D.&L. W.D.S.S./Forms/C. 2118.

# WAR DIARY
## INTELLIGENCE SUMMARY

9th Brigade  
R.F.A.  
Sheet No. 7

| Place | Date | Hour | Summary of Events and Information | Remarks and references to Appendices |
|---|---|---|---|---|
| ARMENTIERES | 18.11.15 | | | |
| | | 10.30am | Some form reported to the fact was reported. The enemy retaliated by firing Rifle into ARMENTIERES and HOUPLINES with "whizz bangs" shrapnel (probably taken from time fuses) and 5.9in guns. It was noticeable that the damage to houses in the neighbourhood was much greater than to those in this shelter neighbourhood. The enemy fire seemed to be by Bde Hdqrs concentrated all the 15 pdr Bde Batts Hq. to explode. The shrubbery round all the afternoon and as it contained very high trees carried a good Hqtchre display. Nearly all the Brigade's telephone communications were destroyed by this heavy explosion. It is estimated that the German fire between 400 and 500 shells into the town. Total number of rounds fired by the Brigade during the day 900. We had the luck not be in the bombardment about 5pm. Completely shutting up the enemy's artillery. A certain amount of trouble has been experienced in the batteries through buffer springs breaking or failing a replacement set and as spares all not carried guns are out of action much longer than need be necessary. | |
| | 19.11.15 | | A very quiet day after yesterday's storm. Maj. Gen. C W Jacob C.B., took over command of the Division. Capt. J M. Strathorne R.A.M.C. joined the Brigade as M.O. vice Lieut. J.P.F. Warren transferred to 14th N. Fusrs. | |
| | 20.11.15 | | | |
| | 21.11.15 | | Comparatively quiet; little artillery fire on German side; replies to do. | by double the amount on our side. |

Army Form C. 211

# WAR DIARY
## or
## INTELLIGENCE SUMMARY.
(Erase heading not required.)

96th Brigade R.F.A.  Sheet No 8.

Instructions regarding War Diaries and Intelligence Summaries are contained in F. S. Regs., Part II. and the Staff Manual respectively. Title pages will be prepared in manuscript.

| Place | Date | Hour | Summary of Events and Information | Remarks and references to Appendices |
|---|---|---|---|---|
| ARMENTIÈRES | 22.11.15 | | Quiet. | |
| | 23.11.15 | | Gen. Jacob inspected the Gun positions of the Brigade, remarking that the men were clean and well kept. | |
| | 24.11.15 | | Quiet. | |
| | 25.11.15 | | The enemy shelled with 4.2" howitzers part of our trenches doing comparatively little damage. | |
| | 26.11.15 | | We retaliated by the fire of A/96 battery and C/97 howitzer battery, a certain amount of damage was done to their trenches and apparently a bomb store was blown up. The next news of the French Periscope to the Brigade from Battery H.Q.'s of the enemy. The information obtained from observation by our F.O.O.'s of the enemy trenches. | |
| | 27.11.15 | | 2/Lt LA CONNOLLY slightly wounded (A. Battery). | |
| | 28.11.15 | | Intermittent shelling of town of ARMENTIÈRES replied to by no result noticed. | |
| | 29.11.15 | | | |
| | 30.11.15 | | | |

96th Bde-RFA.
Vol. 4

131/7911

31st/Hurasion

Army Form C. 2118.

# WAR DIARY
# INTELLIGENCE SUMMARY

of 96th Brigade R.F.A.      Sheet No. 7.

(Erase heading not required.)

| Place | Date | Hour | Summary of Events and Information | Remarks and references to Appendices |
|---|---|---|---|---|
| ARMENTIERES | 1/12/15 to 5/12/15 | | Nothing of importance occurred. The infantry trenches were much affected by the rain. Also some of our gun positions which had to be raised to ground level. Occasional retaliation and counter retaliation. | |
| | 6/12/15 | 5.30 pm | The 4.5 9th H.F. Battery joined the brigade from the Canadian Division in order to assist in minor operation. The position taken up by the battery was just south of the ARMENTIERES–LILLE road in the 23rd Division area (by arrangement with the latter). Battery Commander (of 459th Battery) Capt. LORD ALFRED BROWNE. | |
| | | 6 p.m. | Two H.2 shells fell immediately in rear of gun emplacement of B. Battery causing the following casualties - 1 O.R. killed and 1 O.R. wounded. The latter, including the battery sergeant major, who died whilst being carried to clearing station. | |
| | 7/12/15 | | B. Battery quitted Bde (Capt NANSEN, R.G.A) joined the Brigade being attached to this group, which in the right sector of 21st Division (II Corps), for minor operations, and took up position in CHAPELLE D'ARMENTIERES, firing at a range of about 2200 to German front line trenches. | |
| | 8/12/15 | 12 noon | Wire-cutting by 18 pr. batteries at two points and shelling of CHAU D'HESPEL and WEZ MACQUART by howitzer batteries (C/91 & 459th). Range for wire cutter was be observed was from 2000 to 2500. The shoot on the wire could not be observed owing to indifferent light. | |
| | | 4 pm | C. Battery was shelled by a H.2 battery and received one direct hit on the L.G. of a gun emplacement. This emplacement was roofed with a ballast of still rails' hand over a support - two layers of brick rubble in sand-bags - one layer earth in sand-bags - on top two layers of which rubble in sand-bags. The shell penetrated the sand-bags and exploded below | |

Army Form C. 2118.

# WAR DIARY
## INTELLIGENCE SUMMARY
of 6th Brigade RFA

Sheet No. 10.

(Erase heading not required.)

Instructions regarding War Diaries and Intelligence Summaries are contained in F. S. Regs., Part II. and the Staff Manual respectively. Title pages will be prepared in manuscript.

| Place | Date | Hour | Summary of Events and Information | Remarks and references to Appendices |
|---|---|---|---|---|
| ARMENTIERES | 8.12.15 | 4 pm | a dull raw[?] day. Thanks to the protection the damage done was comparatively slight. Its material the shell did only slight damage being best[?] casualties were O.R. one killed, three wounded. | |
| | 9.12.15 | 12 noon | The 2nd Army Commander (General PLUMER) inspected the wagon line of the Brigade, and being turned-out harnessed up. | |
| | | 2 pm to 3.30 pm | The town of ARMENTIERES was fairly heavily shelled. The wagon lines in PONT DE NIEPPE were also shelled and had to temporarily evacuate their position. In reply to this, the Brigade gave the plan of special retaliation, firing in all some 600 rounds (including about 150 H.E.) Attached Battalion joined in the retaliation as well. The Army Commander expressed his satisfaction at the conduct of the horse and turn-out of the harness and wished it to be conveyed to all ranks. At the same time General JACOB asked the O.C. Brigade (Lt Col R.C. COATES) to express to all ranks that he considered the effect of the shooting on the 8th & 9th Dec. most satisfactory. | |
| | 10.12.15 | 9.20 to 11.30 / 4.15 to 4.45 | Enemy shelled the town of ARMENTIERES at intervals. | |
| | | | Enemy shelled the town again, this time heavily. The Brigade H.Q. (Miller) was hit. Casualties:- an orderly of B. Battery was seriously wounded passing through the town. Brigade H.Q. moved to another part of the town. | |
| | 11.12.15 | | Very quiet day. | |
| | 12.12.15 | | The gun positions of the Brigade were inspected by Brig. Gen. FRANKS, G.O.C. R.A. II Corps. | |
| | 13.12.15 | | | |
| | 14.12.15 | | Quiet. | |

# WAR DIARY
## INTELLIGENCE SUMMARY.

Army Form C. 2118.

96th Brigade H.Q. — Sheet No. 11.

| Place | Date | Hour | Summary of Events and Information | Remarks and references to Appendices |
|---|---|---|---|---|
| ARMENTIERES | 15/16.11 | | A cutting out expedition having been ordered for the night 15/16" when undertaken was advised and was undertaken by the 2nd Battalion of the Rifle Brigade which consists of 96th Brigade to which is attached 2/97 Bty R.F.A. and 459 Battery (How.) (Canadian Division). The object was to destroy enemy's salient and machine gun emplacements (probably machine gun emplacements elsewhere on the line from which fire could be brought to bear on the attack, to cut wire at the point of attack and in other places to deceive the enemy. Two batteries were told off for the actual wire cutting at the point of attack being given to 25 yard broad each. One battery cut the front and cut morsels in about a foot broad at a range of 2000 yds. The other battery concentrated its fire and cut a clean front 9 yard broad at a range of 2600 yds. This wire was cut by the infantry in this attack and was reported as excellent. The attack took place at 3.15 a.m. night 15/16". The object being to kill and capture enemy and bring back to this line and roughly take 5 minute for this enterprise to move from our front line to the German parapet. Wire being cut at 3.15 this barrage was made which synchronised an artillery barrage was begun at 3.15 this barrage was made along the trenches that the infantry were to find. Appendix H | |

# WAR DIARY
## INTELLIGENCE SUMMARY

6th Brigade R.F.A.  Sheet No. 12

| Place | Date | Hour | Summary of Events and Information | Remarks and references to Appendices |
|---|---|---|---|---|
| ARMENTIERES | 16.4.15 | | This barrage was most effective & completely nullified the cutting of our wire in parts from any possibility of attack. The infantry attacked were all lights with all our fire and said that they felt absolutely safe with it. Gun from any enemy attack. The only communication with the attacking party which was retained by the 21st Division during the operations was in fact by the Infantry Brigade in charge (a Lucien D.V.) to our front line trenches (a Lucien D.V.) & thence to their excellent subterranean railway in their most successful mine cutting by A Battery 2nd Lieut C.S. KING was awarded a Military Cross for orders for night operations see Appendix A. During the day operations C Battery was shelled towards in top of the guns emplacements slightly damaging the gun and killing 3 gunners and wounding the No 1. and two gunners. Congratulatory messages from Army Commander 2nd Army Commander were received | Appendix A |
| | 16.4.15 | | On the conclusion of the above minor enterprise the H59 Battery was returned to the Canadian Corps and C/98 was sent back to rest for ten days in Corps Rest Area, NOOTE BOOM. | T. Ridin D. C. D. r E |

# WAR DIARY or INTELLIGENCE SUMMARY

96th Brigade R.F.A. Sheet No. 13.

| Place | Date | Hour | Summary of Events and Information | Remarks and references to Appendices |
|---|---|---|---|---|
| ARMENTIERES | 7.10.15 | | Quiet | |
| | 8.10.15 | | Intermittent shelling | |
| | 9.10.15 | 6.45am | The German laid up five particular first line trenches at the MUSHROOM (I.1.c. N.W.Sh.36.N.W.) Another mine was blown up alongside the first one ten yards further up the Epinoy. When the first mine exploded the S.O.S. signal was given from the trenches — A/96 opened fire in 15 seconds. B/96 and C/97 further in 15 seconds. | |
| | | 9 am | The enemy shelled some 500 rounds in 15 minutes in support and CHAPELLE D'ARMENTIERES C/97 covering in front a fair amount of the shells There were no casualties in our lines except that a wagon was hit. | |
| | | | During the night following B/96 were called on several times to support our trenches. A/96 and B/96 were called to remember the whole of the Brigade was called upon to Heavy fire all day but at night the Enemy made no attack on the English, and fire was continued until the 9c. Infantry Battalion reported that he was satisfied. Congratulations of our General the Brigade. | |
| | 10.10.15 | | Fairly quiet during the day. During the night R/95 was called on to support working parties at Der Oaken. | |
| | 11.10.15 | 7.10pm | A presentation by the 91st Brigade in which this Brigade assisted R. = B/96 were called upon to assist the infantry in repairing along | Appendix F |

2353  Wt. W.2544/1454  700,000  5/15  D. D. & L.  A.D.S.S./Forms/C.2118.

# WAR DIARY or INTELLIGENCE SUMMARY

**Army Form C. 2118.**

Place: **ARMENTIERES**

| Date | Hour | Summary of Events and Information | Remarks and references to Appendices |
|---|---|---|---|
| 22.12.15 / 23.12.15 | | Bombing party. CHAPELLE D'ARMENTIERES and LILLE ROAD persistently shelled by the enemy. | |
| 24.12.15 | | A moderately quiet day. There was a considerable amount of firing on our right. LILLE ROAD was again rather heavily shelled. | |
| 25.12.15 | | Having received orders from Divl Army Commander not to fire except the situation the day was comparatively quiet. The 2/5th Durham on our right however fired a lot which was evidently not cared to by the enemy firing on I. I. d (Map 36 NW 1/20000) from 11 am to noon. Our batts 14g situated in ston square had some narrow escapes. A comparatively quiet day. C 9b returned to its former position this evening. | |
| 26.12.15 | | Bombardment of enemy's front line and support trenches apposite MUSHROOM | Appendix I |
| 27.12.15 | | I 11 C (Map 36 NW 1/20000) was carried out the effect being to do as much damage as possible to give that it probably some damage was done the majority of trenches and lets clear of new recently fielding about. The enemy retaliated vigorously & immediately against A196. Q hundred straight the batty was heavily & in volumes as possible to 6.0 - 4.2" and 5.9" shells fell all round it, within a few yards. The only means however were two women [unclear] who were could into a place of safety under heavy shell fire by Sergt DUNSTAN and Gunner WILSON. One gun emplacement was hit and started burning, as the heavy fire was so intense the ammunition was again to the emplacement could not be withdrawn. Consequently it caught fire and | |

Army Form C. 2118.

# WAR DIARY
## INTELLIGENCE SUMMARY.
*(Erase heading not required.)*

96th Brigade R.F.A.  Sheet No. 15.

| Place | Date | Hour | Summary of Events and Information | Remarks and references to Appendices |
|---|---|---|---|---|
| | 27.12.15 | | Most of the cartridges exploded singly at short intervals. It is estimated that no simultaneous explosion of the whole of the Ammunition in the wagon took place. | |
| | 28.12.15 | | The section A/96 moved out to Rest-camp at NOOTE BOOM. | |
| | 29.12.15 | | Quiet | |
| | 30.12.15 | | | |
| | 31.12.15 | | Also quiet. One section of B/96 moved into a position allotted to subtable communication trenches in 23rd Division area (at salient R.w.E. DU BOIS - I 21 8 6 in. 2½" Map 36 N.W. 20000) and one section of D/96 moved up into position vacated by A/96, to be able to harbour enemy front parapet at I 26 d 3.4 in order to facilitate mills trench 23rd Division in their minor enterprise against I 26 c 8.4 (enemy salient) Reg. retaliation was carried out by above sections. 9/96 was also called upon to assist in this Scheme. | Appendix I |
| | Midnight 31/12/15 1/1/16 | | We wish the readers of this Diary a more pleasant ending to the coming year although he may lie there favourably situated that we are at present. | |

R.C. Walter
Lieut. and Adjt.
96th F.A. B^de

### 96th Bde Operation Orders No 2.   "A"

Reference Trench Map No 12.

1. Infantry will assault night 15/16th inst commencing at 3.15 a.m.

   They will occupy the enemy trenches for 20 minutes and will then return to their own trenches. They will therefore start back at about 3.35 a.m.

   The fire of all Batteries will be continued until the order to stop firing is received, which will be given 10 minutes after the Infantry are all back.

   Batteries will therefore expect to receive the order to stop firing at about 3.45 a.m. The order will be sent by Telephone and also by runner, if possible to B/94, B/96 and C/97. These runners must report to 2/Lieut. Nash, Orderly officer 96 Bde RFA at 9 p.m. 15th inst. at SQUARE FARM.

2. After "Stop Firing" Batteries will stand by until further orders in case of a counter attack.

3. Wire Cutting and Bombardment will commence at 10.35 a.m 15th inst and be continued at intervals as in Table A.

4. For Barrage during Infantry attack night 15/16th inst see Table B.

2.

5. The Barrage of Fire will commence exactly at 3.18 a.m. night 15/16th inst. The greatest care must be taken that it commences at that minute and must not be opened before. Rate of fire Section Fire 15 seconds.

6. 2/Lieut. Denvir C/96 will go forward with Col. Howard Commanding the Assaulting Infantry with Telephone and Operator. The Wire should be rolled round stout twine. About 300 yards will be wanted.

7. A/96 will fire a few rounds on night 13/14th on front line trenches opposite to ascertain difference between night and day ranges and will notify the results to Brigade Head Quarters.

B de Melle Lieut RFA
Adjt 96 Bde RFA.

## Table A.

| Time Table | Unit | Target | Shrap | H.E. | Object |
|---|---|---|---|---|---|
| 10.35 am to 11.05 am | A/96 B/96 | I.11.c.6.5 to a point 50 yards South of 6.5. | 300 300 | | Make a gap 50 yards in enemy Wire. A/96 right 25 yards B/96 left 25 yards |
| 12.10pm to 12.40pm | C/97 | I.11.c.6.5 to a point 50 yards South of 6.5. | | 100 | Make a gap in enemy wire and parapet. |
| 1pm to 1.30pm or until wire cutting is complete and as per Amm Table is expended. | B/94 C/97 459 B? C/96 | I.17.a.2.8, 25 yards S a N. I.16.b.5.0. I.17.a.2.8 & I.16.b.9.3. I.11.c.6.5 to I.5.c.7.1. | 200 100 | 100 40 100 100 | Cut wire & damage parapet. Destroy M.G. Emplacements " " To catch enemy on the move especially from Salient. |
| 10.35am onwards | D/96 | Railway Salient and Trench South Side. | 100 | 200 | To destroy emplacements. |

## Table B.

Barrage. 3.18 a.m. 16th mt at least until 3.45 a.m.

| Time Table | Unit | Target | Shrap | H.E. | Object |
|---|---|---|---|---|---|
|  | C/97 | I.17.b.3.6 and I.16.b.5.0 |  | 120 | To destroy supports & make a screen of smoke & dust in houses |
|  | 459 By | I.17.a.2.8 and I.17.a.4.6 |  | 120 | To block trenches and destroy M.G. emplacements. |
|  | D/96 | I.11.a.6.0 to I.11.a.3.2 | 100 | 200 | The lyddite to be used to enfilade the trench. |
| 3.18 a.m. | A/96 | I.17.a.2.8 to I.11.c.7.1 | 200 | 100 | Shrapnel Barrage. None of these rounds to be short. |
|  | B/96 | I.11.c.7.1 to I.11.c.9.5 | 200 | 100 |  |
|  | B/94 | I.11.c.9.5 to Railway | 200 | 100 |  |
|  | C/96 | Railway to I.5.c.7.1 | 200 | 100 |  |

To A/96.
B/96
C/96
B/94.

**SECRET.**

It is to be understood that the Barrage of Fire Table B is to be "Rate of Fire Intense" and that it must be kept up incessantly until the Infantry return to their trenches which it is supposed, will be about 3.45 a.m.

I will endeavour to let you know directly the Infantry have returned.

14-12-15.

B. G. Melle Lieut RFA
Adjt 96 Bde RFA.

**MESSAGES AND SIGNALS.**    Army Form C. 2121.

TO: 96 Bde (Will you please repeat to 104th Bde: RFA.

Sender's Number: G.M. 62   Day of Month: Sixteenth   AAA

Commander Second Army congratulates all ranks on success of this mornings enterprise AAA His appreciation to be expressed to all those engaged AAA ~~addressed~~ ~~96 Bde repeated 104 Bde~~ ~~AAA~~ D/ros.

From: 31 DIV ART
Time: Noon

**CONFIDENTIAL.** D 73.

"G"

~~9th Brigade R.F.A.~~
~~45 Brigade R.F.A.~~
~~96th Brigade R.F.A.~~
~~1st Canadian Heavy Battery~~
~~Trench Mortars~~

The Army Commander has expressed a wish that fire will not be opened by us on Christmas day. It is to be clearly understood however that the Germans must not be allowed to take liberties and that if fire is opened by them the usual forms of retaliation must be employed.

The Army Commander has sent a Christmas card wishing The Divisional Artillery a Happy Christmas.

Craig
Capt RFA
Bde Maj. 21 Div Art

24.12.15.
Sent under B233 all units
7.45 pm

BM.31/7.

..............................

       Herewith Report on Operations carried out yesterday. The G.O.C., 21st Division has asked me to convey to all the Batteries which took part in the Operations his thanks, and his appreciation for their able assistance.

       To this, I wish to add my hearty congratulations to all ranks of the 21st Divisional Artillery for the steady and effective fire which was brought to bear by the Batteries which contributed so much to the success of the enterprise.

                              R. Wellesley.

H.Q. 21 Div. Art.               Brigadier-General.
16th December 1915.   Commanding, 21st Divisional Arty.

Officer Commanding
96th Ja/Bde

The following letter has been received by the Brigadier-General Commanding 21st Divisional Artillery, from The General Officer Commanding 2nd Corps:-

" I want to congratulate you and your Gunners most
" heartily on the fine work they did on Wednesday
" last in connection with the MUSHROOM Enterprise.
" I am told that the shooting was first rate, and
" it is beyond question that the Enterprise could
" not have been carried out successfully without
" the splendid preparation and support of the Guns.
" The Army Commander wishes me specially to
" congratulate you on his behalf.
" Please tell all your people how much this good
" work is appreciated, and how well the Infantry
" know how much they are indebted to the Artillery
" for their support.
" It is satisfactory to think that the Boschos got
" a good shake up ".

The above letter should be communicated to all ranks.

R. Wellesley.
Brigadier-General.
1918-12-1915.   Commanding 21st Divisional Artillery.

SPECIAL BRIGADE ORDER

BY

Brigadier General E.R.Hill
Commanding 63rd Infantry Brigade.
------------------------------------------

THURSDAY.
16th December 1915.

12. The following message is published for information:-

" Army Commander congratulates all ranks on success of this
mornings enterprise and His appreciation to be expressed
to all those engaged."

The Brigadier wishes to add his congratulations and to
express his appreciation of the excellent manner in which
the enterprise was carried out by the 8th Bn. Somerset L.I.
ably supported by 96th F.A. Brigade.
He also wishes to express his appreciation of the steadiness
of the 4th Middlesex Regiment and 10th York and Lancs Regiment
under heavy Artillery Fire.

*for War Diary*

A.G.MACDONALD. Major.

Brigade Major.
63rd Infantry Brigade.

"C" Form (Duplicate).    Army Form C. 2123.

## MESSAGES AND SIGNALS.

| | Charges to Pay. £ s. d. | Office Stamp. |
|---|---|---|

Service Instructions.

Handed in at ____ Office 10.0 m. Received 10.17 m.

TO: Div Art

| Sender's Number | Day of Month | In reply to Number | AAA |
|---|---|---|---|
| G.306 | 21 | | |

The Army commander is very pleased to hear of the success of the operations of the troops of Twentyfirst Divn early this morning aaa round 63rd Inf Bde aaa 7th Sqn LI aaa Div Art

96th Brigade R.M.

For Information.

Stough Capt.
BM 21 WR.

21.XII.15.

FROM PLACE & TIME: Twentyfirst Divn 9.45 pm

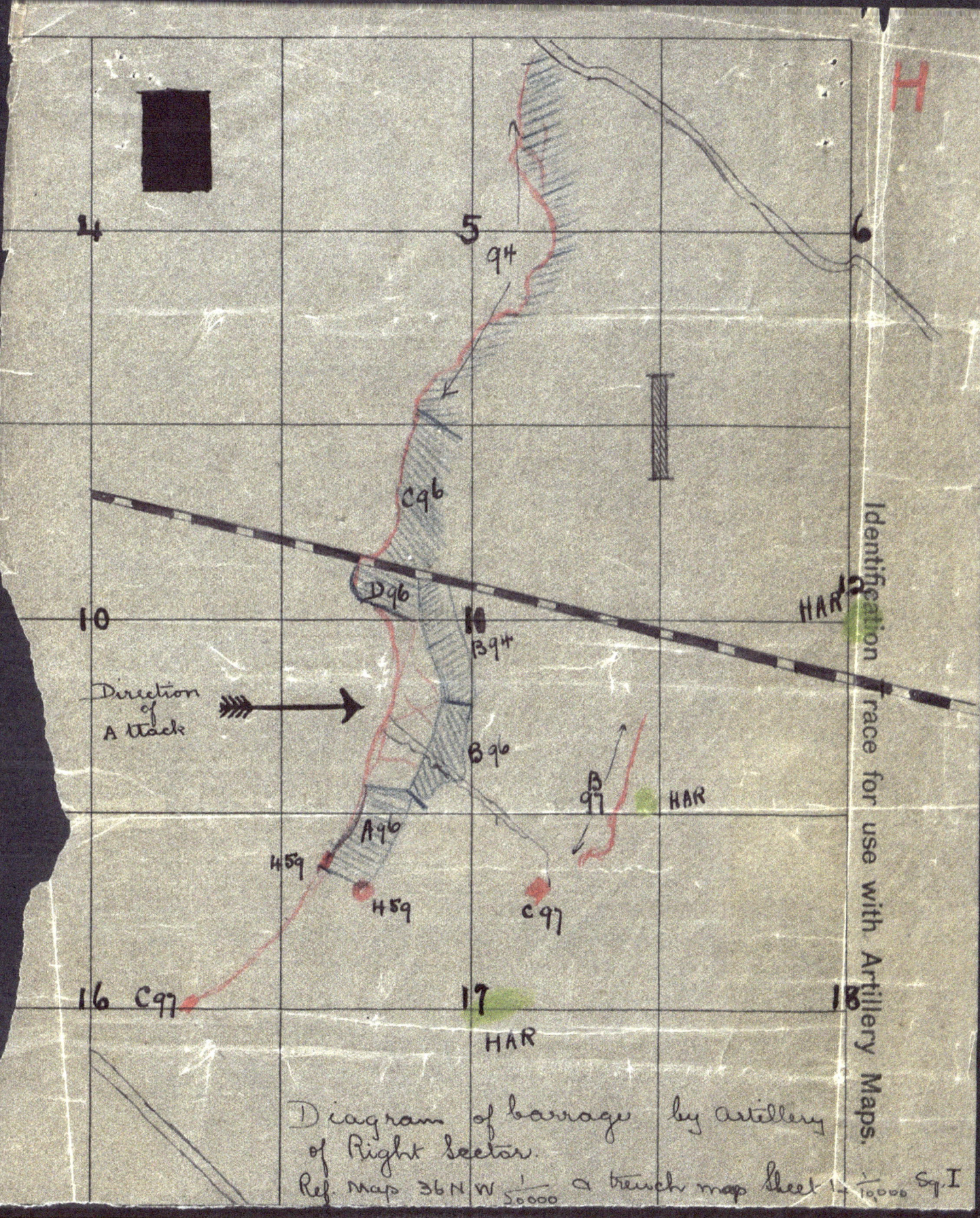

**SECRET**

96th Bde Orders (Operation) No 5.
Reference 10,000 Trench Map No 12.   26-12-15.

1. A Bombardment of Enemy's Front Line and Support Trenches opposite the MUSHROOM will be carried out on the 27th inst.

   The object of the Bombardment is to do as much damage as possible to the Enemy's Parapet and Mine Shaft and block his Communication Trenches.

2. During the morning of the 27th inst Batteries will carry out a careful registration of Enemy's Front Line and Support Trenches at the following hours:
   A/96 — 9.30 to 10.0 am    B/94  10.30 to 11.0 am
   B/96 — 10.0 am to 10.30 am   C/97  11.0 to 11.30 am

3. The Bombardment will commence at 12.45 pm and continue until the ammunition allotted has been expended. Rate of fire to be slow and deliberate. For tasks see Table "A".

   C/96 and D/96 will, if required, fire on retaliation points in rear, on receipt of orders. If these orders cannot be sent the O.C.'s these Batteries will act on their own initiative.

4. Reports to be sent in to 96 Bde HQ at end of operations as to results.

5. Acknowledge by Telephone.

Copies to. H.Q. A/96, B/96, C/96, D/96, B/94, C/97.

P. Smelle Lieut RFA
Adjt 96 Bde RFA.

## Table "A"

| Unit | Target | Object | Ammunition 18 Pdr. Shrap | H.E | 4.5 |
|---|---|---|---|---|---|
| A/96 | I.17.a.2.8 to I.11.c.7.1 | Shell support and front line Trenches with HE and fire Shrapnel down Comm. Trenches. | 200 | 100 | |
| B/96 | I.11.c.7.1 to I.11.c.9.5 | Ditto. | 200 | 100 | |
| B/94 | I.11.c.9.5 to I.11.a.6.0 | Ditto | 200 | 100 | |
| C/97 | I.17.a.2.8 to I.11.c.6.8 | Damage Parapet of Support and front line Trenches. | | | 140 |

"J"

25th Division Minor Operation in conjunction with 71st Div.

## 96 Bde Operation Orders No. 6.    30-12-15.

1. The 9th Yorks with party RE will raid Salient at I.21.b.4.4.

   The 10th N. Fusiliers will raid Salient at I.26.c.8.1.

2. Gas will be used on the flanks of the raids if wind suitable, from I.15.d.6.4 and I.26.b.2.8. Orders for the gas will be given direct from Divisional Headquarters.

3. The two raids will take place simultaneously working by the clock (Signal Time).

   Time Table will be as follows:-

   Time 0.0. Infantry assaults points in German Line.
   " 0.3. Artillery barrage of fire on flanks and behind German Trenches.
   " 0.3. Gas on flanks of attack if wind suitable.
   " 0.15. Infantry and RE move back to our lines.

4. Date and Zero Hour will be sent later.

— TASKS —

| Time | Unit | Object | Rate of Fire | Amm. G. |
|---|---|---|---|---|
| 0.3 to 0.20 | B/96 | Enfilade Support Trench and Front Trench at I.21.b.6½.2½ and I.21.b.6.1 | Section Fire 20 Secs. | 5/ Shrap. |
| 0.20 till Stop is ordered | " | " | Section Fire 30 Secs. | Up 16 100 Rds. |

Copies. 71 Div. B/96, C/96, D/96, & H.Q.

| Time | Unit | Object | Rate of Fire | Amount |
|---|---|---|---|---|
| 0.13 to 0.20 and then STOP. | C/96 (one Section) | Bombard Front Parapet I.16.b.5.0 | Section fire 20 secs. | 250 Shrap 250 HE. |
| 0.13 to 0.20 and then STOP | D/96 (one Section) | Bombard Front Parapet. I.16.d.1/2.3. | Section fire 20 secs. | 250 Shrap 250 HE |

In addition to the above the following tasks will be carried out during the day previous.
This day will be notified later.

| Time | Unit | Object | Rate of Fire | Amount |
|---|---|---|---|---|
| ? | C/96 | Wire Cutting 20 yards. I.16.b.5.0 | Deliberate | 200 Shrapnel |
| ? | D/96 | Wire Cutting 20 yards I.16.d.1.3. | Deliberate | 200 Shrapnel |

<u>ACKNOWLEDGE</u>
30-12-15.

BG Mellu Capt RFA.
Adjt 96 Bde RFA.

To B/96. C/96. D/96.

With reference to the Minor Operation to be carried out in conjunction with the 23rd Division.

(1) The date of the Operation will be 1st January 1916.

(2) The hour of zero is 1.30 a.m. The moon rises at 3.33 a.m.

(3) The O.C. 104th Bde. RFA has been instructed to compare watches with you during the day of the 31st December 1915.

(4) You will not be required to do any wire-cutting on the day of the operation. (C o D)

(5) Acknowledge by wire.

B/ Mells Capt RFA
Adjt 96 Bde RFA.

21st Divisional Artillery.

---

96th BRIGADE R. F. A.

JANUARY 1916.

Army Form C. 2118.

# WAR DIARY
## INTELLIGENCE SUMMARY.
*(Erase heading not required.)*

96th Brigade R.F.A.  Sheet No. 16.

Instructions regarding War Diaries and Intelligence Summaries are contained in F. S. Regs., Part II. and the Staff Manual respectively. Title pages will be prepared in manuscript.

| Place | Date | Hour | Summary of Events and Information | Remarks and references to Appendices |
|---|---|---|---|---|
| ARMENTIERES | 1.1.16 | | Quiet days | |
| | 2.1.16 | | For a considerable time during the middle of the day B/94 battery was very heavily shelled — no damage however was done to equipment. H, 2, and 5.9" batteries took part in the shelling. B/94 might act to their sunken line the sunken lane. | |
| | 3.1.16 | | | |
| | 4.1.16 | | Nothing of interest. | |
| | 5.1.16 | | | |
| | 6.1.16 | 7am | Enemy bombarded trenches 69, 70 T and burned the MUSHROOM I.11.C.2.5. (map 36 N.W. 1/20000). We retaliated with all batteries. A Battery retired from rest area at NOOTE BOOM and took up B/94 position at I.3.C.4.1. B/94 moved out to rest area at NOOTE BOOM. | |
| | 7.1.16 | | | |
| | 8.1.16 | | As the Germans on their side of the crater have been during the last few days putting up inwhwod retirement and machinery trenches generally dragoning at this point, it was decided to try and knock down this cover. A.B (in shaded) | |

[sketch showing A-B line at 36°30′, with area marked "British" and arrow pointing S, and "MUSHROOM"]

Trench mortars (2") were employed together with 4.97 (4.5") to carry this out, A/96 (18 P) living hire to keep the enemy which down algo. It was General ... considerable damage was done to the reflections. Appendix A.
The enemy retaliating on the MUSHROOM. (A.B)

Army Form C. 2118.

# WAR DIARY
## INTELLIGENCE SUMMARY.
*(Erase heading not required.)*

96th Brigade R.F.A. Sheet 5/7.

Instructions regarding War Diaries and Intelligence Summaries are contained in F.S. Regs. Part II. and the Staff Manual respectively. Title pages will be prepared in manuscript.

| Place | Date | Hour | Summary of Events and Information | Remarks and references to Appendices |
|---|---|---|---|---|
| ARMENTIERES | 9.1.16 10.1.16 | | Quiet day. | |
| | 11.1.16 | 10 a.m. | D/96 was heavily shelled. The enemy fire lasted some three hours the rate of fire being rapid at first and afterwards slackening off, and found a moment and two to one round every ten minutes. The total number of shell fires is estimated at 105 heavy shell including 4.2", 5.9", 8", and 15 c.m. Among the pieces picked up was one of what was apparently an airburn piercing projectile. No damage was done to either our equipment although shell fell all round the guns. A minor enterprise holding liesul aimed on the left sector about PONT BALLOT C 39 c 4/2 9/2. A bombardment and wire cutting was ordered for this hour. The actual attack was timed for 11.15 p.m. i.e. 30 minutes before the moon set. The brigade stood by for retaliation and counter battery work but our assistance was not required. | Appendix A |
| | 12.1.16 13.1.16 | | Quiet day. Some 40 rounds of 80 m/m ammunition were fired into CHAPELLE D'ARMENTIERES otherwise everything was quiet in our sector. | |
| | 14.1.16 | | Again the only unit of interest was the 80 m/m gun in CHAPELLE D'ARMENTIERES. This gun seems to be very troublesome in its effects. | |
| | 15.1.16 | | In the morning a 15 c.m. Howitzer put 16 rounds into D Battery. Might of these were duds and no damage was done. | |

A.D.S.S./Forms/C.2118.

Army Form C. 2118.

# WAR DIARY
# INTELLIGENCE SUMMARY.
*(Erase heading not required.)*

96th & A Brigade RFA                    Phil No 16

| Place | Date | Hour | Summary of Events and Information | Remarks and references to Appendices |
|---|---|---|---|---|
| ARMENTIERES | 15.1.16 | | | Map 36 NW |
| | | 4.40pm | A Battery fired on a small bridge, served by a known carrier screw. One of the rounds hit a dug-out seen causing an explosion. (J 11 c 6.7) The enemy put some twenty rounds into the town and later put one or two rounds in every half hour until about 1 a.m. The 2nd Army Heavy Group retaliated on LILLE but this Brigade did not fire. | |
| | | | In the Gazette of 1.1.16 the following officers and men of this Brigade were "mentioned in despatches":— LT. COL. R. E. COATES, D.S.O. MAJOR T. MCGOWAN, LIEUT. S.D. TIMSON, LIEUT. C.S. KING, No. 30937 CORPORAL R.W.I. COOK and GUNNER No. 23017 GUNNER T. TAYLOR. In the London Gazette of 13.1.16 the following honours were published:— Companion of the D.S.O. Major T. MACGOWAN (D Battery). | |
| | 16.1.16 | | | |
| | 17.1.16 | 5.30am | Battery of intent. | |
| | | | We cooperated with an aeroplane for the first time in the war. One of our aeroplanes which was flying very low for special observation was heavily fired on by hostile infantry. Three of our batteries opened fire and silenced in turn most of the line of rifles and machine guns. The enemy put about 30 shells into the town but the remainder of the night was quiet. | |
| | | 7.4pm | | |

# WAR DIARY
## or
## INTELLIGENCE SUMMARY

Army Form C. 2118.

Instructions regarding War Diaries and Intelligence Summaries are contained in F. S. Regs., Part II. and the Staff Manual respectively. Title pages will be prepared in manuscript.

_____ 4th Brigade R.F.A. _____ Abt ___

(Erase heading not required.)

| Place | Date | Hour | Summary of Events and Information | Remarks and references to Appendices |
|---|---|---|---|---|
| ARMENTIERES | 18.1.16 | | No event of interest. | |
| | 19.1.16 | 9.30 a.m. | The enemy started shelling C Battery of 1st Bde. and continued throughout the day until 4.30 p.m. with an interval of 1 hour (presumably for lunch) in the middle of the day. A little shrapnel ranged the enemy's batteries at the start of the shoot was used early in the afternoon. Altogether about 30 - 21 cm., 30 - 15 m. and 150 - 10.5 cm. shell in all. Fortunately innumerable 77 mm. shell were fired. There were no casualties to personnel, but the gun pits were damaged as follows:- one gun-chamber roof and sandbag protection destroyed, two guns slightly damaged but can still be fired. Three men no doubt hiding in the gun-chambers were buried by sandbags and timber, but escaped without injury. I consider that the enemy must have known that they were firing 15 of the rounds, that they are including 15 to 6 P.M. They must have been in their zone in a place a little over 200 yds. in length and width which would never be suspected by 6 when view issued to the battery position. This may not be the case (they may have withdrawn) as we have found that it is the line entrance of the enemy to day, releasing much on a battery position, as left when that Battery has been heavily shelled during the day. Any men who may be working at the position...

#353 Wt. W2544/1434 100,000 5/15 D.D. & L. T. Co.Ltd.  A.D.S.S./Forms/C. 2118.

Army Form C. 2113.

# WAR DIARY
## INTELLIGENCE SUMMARY.
*(Erase heading not required.)*

95th Brigade R.F.A.   About No 30

| Place | Date | Hour | Summary of Events and Information | Remarks and references to Appendices |
|---|---|---|---|---|
| ARMENTIERES | 19.1.16 | 10 a.m. | When the shelling first started in the morning No. 34559 Gnr A. JONES with great bravery under heavy shellfire went to each gun emplacement there being widely scattered, and removed and brought in all its aid sights, making two journeys to do this. He did this because he knew, from previous occasions, that the enemy invited hostile shelling there sights were even with limited hostile shelling. Generally unseen. | |
| | 20.1.16 | | 6 Battery unearthed than damaged guns and withdrew to their wagon line, pending the preparation of a new position. Nothing of interest. | M.A.P - 50,000 36 N.W |
| | 21.1.16 22.1.16 23.1.16 | | D 196 for enfiladed PRMESQUES ROAD (I '7 and I 24) at intervals during the day – some 50 rounds being fired. This is done most days in the road is much by the enemy. B 196 (one section) cut the wire in front of its southern sap out to Mud Crater. One gun was shortly unable to continue its shooting. The 6/c B. Battery unfortunately did not confine the 6.W.R. gun which was shortly after cut a entering number of rounds were wasted. The infantry expressed themselves as satisfied with the wire cut. | Appendix A |
| | 24.1.16 | | The Engineers were broken by the shells. About 300 shrapnel + 4 yards of cow hung down. | |

A.D.S.S./Forms/C. 2118.

# WAR DIARY
## INTELLIGENCE SUMMARY.

96th Brigade HQ

| Place | Date | Hour | Summary of Events and Information | Remarks and references to Appendices |
|---|---|---|---|---|
| ARMENTIERES | 24.1.16 | | and 50 H.E. were used. This morning includes round just to our Another bomb in the wire opposite the Northern sap out to the mine Crater (as a blind to its mouth). | |
| | 25.1.16 | 9pm | Cyclist made an attempt to enter the German sap this ap (to the craters) which is not more than 30 yds from our sap in the near side of the crater. They however failed to reach really with a strong bombing party in (the sap) and they withdrew from the marginal contest. | |
| | 26.1.16 | | Heavy shelling of infantry trenches on both sides. Afternoon quiet. | |
| | 27.1.16 | | Major Rains's battery (27) tonight put strings rounds of green battery much worried on our infilade to front. A few hundred shells were dropped all over the back but dug practically no damage. Some fifty rounds fell however 91/96 batts. battern but beyond wothering our men (by the first shell) no damage was done. | |
| | | 11.40pm | The division on our right was heavily shelled and asked for assistance which was given by A/9/... | |
| | 28.1.16 | | Orders were received to make a change in the Telephone by running the connection between the "L" + "E" terminal and (to have that also to lay the line back to its earth pin from the front trenches) giving the same course as and parallel to the front trench and using the actual repair being | |

Army Form C. 2118.

# WAR DIARY
## INTELLIGENCE SUMMARY.

(Erase heading not required.)

| Place | Date | Hour | Summary of Events and Information | Remarks and references to Appendices |
|---|---|---|---|---|
| | | | 4th Bde R.F.A. | |
| ARMENTIERES | 6.1.16 | | Received that the enemy could still hear our telephone message. | |
| | 31.1.16 | | C/9b moved into their new positions which they had been preparing during the preceding days. Preparation was asked for by the 2.S.S. Division however to assist in cutting out expedition. The Germans wanted her + having wanted her + having see its initial stage that the expedition was on received orders that the expedition was off. | |

R.C. Coats
Major R.F.A
Cmdg 9b R.F.A Bde

To A/96, C/97.   Operation Order No 7.   7-1-16   **A**

I. The following bombardment will be commenced tomorrow, the 8th inst.

| Time fire to be opened | Unit | Objective | Amount Amn not to exceed |
|---|---|---|---|
| 11.0 a.m. | A/96 | Fire on Enemy's Trenches at I.11.c, at Intense Fire 30 seconds during Bombardment. 50% H.E. | 250 rounds. |
| 11.0 a.m. | C/97 | Shell Trenches I.11.c.4/5.1 to I.11.c.6/7. To destroy Sandbag Works on East side of crater at I.11.c.8.3½. | 50 rounds. 100 rounds. |

II. Trench Mortars will also be employed.

III. ACKNOWLEDGE.

B. Melle Capt RFA.
Adjt 96 Bde RFA.

## 96th Bde Operation Orders No 8.    A1

1. 21st Div. Cyclists will attack the enemy's trenches at the Craters at 9.50 pm on Jan 25th. The operation is expected to be completed by 10.15 pm.

2. A/96 and D/96 will be prepared to fire on their night lines. B/96 will be prepared to fire in front of the MUSHROOM. C/97 will have 2 guns on South side of Railway Salient, one gun on I.17.a.3.6 and one gun on I.16.b.9.3.

   None of these Batteries will open fire without direct orders from this office except B/96 as it is proposed that this enterprise should be done quietly and without gun fire.

3. If ordered to open fire however, this will be at Section Fire 30 seconds, care being taken to search enemy parapet except opposite MUSHROOM, as it is likely that Germans may flee into "NO MANS LAND."

4. On the 24th inst B/96 will cut wire North and South of the Craters at points already described.

   O.C. B/96 will obtain a report from the officer concerned that the wire has been cut to his satisfaction.

Amt. Shrapnel 200. H.E. 50

5.  FOO of B/96 will be with Major HAY Divisional Cyclists during night operations. OC B/96 will arrange telephone communications between his FOO and the Battery. He will also arrange for Tapping-in Stations as required.

6.  Reports to be sent in immediately as to result of Wire cutting, and during and immediately after the "Night" Operation by all FOOs in a position to observe.

7.  ACKNOWLEDGE.

Copies to A/96
B/96
D/96
C/97
N.O.

B.H. Mellu Capt RFA.
Adjt 96 Bde RFA

96th Bde. Operation Order No 7. — 10-1-16. **B**

# SECRET.

I. The 62nd Inf. Bde. will attack PONT BALLOT Salient at 11.15pm on the 11th inst.
   The Infantry will occupy the trenches for 20 minutes.

II. A Bombardment and Wire Cutting will commence at 11am. on the 11th inst.

III. The Batteries detailed below will register enemy batteries as shown, and will be ready to open fire on them by night should they shell our trenches.
   C/96 on    J.7.a.4½.5.
   D/96  "    T.24.b.6.1.
   C/97  "    T.23.b.8.2 to 8.9½.
   A/96 } will be prepared to take on objectives
   B/94 } in their zones as may be ordered.

IV. B/94 will register on Trenches opposite 67 and 68 tomorrow.

V. ACKNOWLEDGE.

Copies to HQ.
   C/96.
   D/96.                AG Mellé Capt RFA.
   A/96.                Adjt. 96 Bde RFA.
   B/94.
   C/97.

21st Divisional Artillery.

95th BRIGADE R. F. A.

FEBRUARY 1916.

# WAR DIARY
## INTELLIGENCE SUMMARY

96th Brigade R.F.A. Sheet No 33

| Place | Date | Hour | Summary of Events and Information | Remarks and references to Appendices |
|---|---|---|---|---|
| ARMENTIERES | 1.2.16<br>2.2.16<br>4.2.16<br>5.2.16 | | No event of importance. | Sheet 36 N.W<br>1/20,000 |
| | 5/6.2.16 | | A Rifle Battery observed fire from B.13.a.4.8 on our position I.24.c.2.6. (little damage in regard to our battery on reserves in rear). Shells were not very satisfactory as regards its stability in its target. Warning was given at about 300 yds our aid to stability of the target. A nets system of holding the trenches was adopted in the Division. The Divisional front was divided into two sectors instead of three and front line trenches in each sector were held by two battalions in each sector of the A Coy and C Coy covering the right sector respectively of the B Coy and D Coy covering the R.F.A. in the event of urgent calls. This alteration of gun & R.F.A. in the position of duty called for F.O.O's necessitated certain changes in its position of the F.O.O's. | |
| | 7.2.16<br>11.2.16 | | No unusual activity in this sector noted during this period on either side. | |
| | 12.2.16 | 2.5pm | Very violent bombardment by the enemy of trenches in the Right sector and many casualties in rear. The enemy appeared to be firing its cut our wire and it the shop much damaged by shell fire. The F.O.O. of B/96 thinking its enemy were about to attack gave the S.O.S. call. This intense bombardment lasted about 20 minutes. | |
| | 13.2.16 | 9.15pm | The enemy again bombarded our front trench for a short time where bombarded steadily its whole day. Trench B's was heavily shelled with field guns; field howitzer and 15cm howitzer. A shell fell into the officers' mess of A/96 but luckily it did not explode and three men who casualties all escaped injuries also front line trenches were shelled by in. The area in rear of our | |

Army Form C. 2118.

# WAR DIARY
## or
## INTELLIGENCE SUMMARY.

96th Infantry Brigade R.F.A. (Erase heading not required.) Sheet No 24

Instructions regarding War Diaries and Intelligence Summaries are contained in F. S. Regs., Part II. and the Staff Manual respectively. Title pages will be prepared in manuscript.

| Place | Date | Hour | Summary of Events and Information | Remarks and references to Appendices |
|---|---|---|---|---|
| ARMENTIERES | 14.2.16 | | Trenches were also heavily shelled by the enemy. | |
| | 15.2.16 | | Quiet day. | |
| | | | Quiet day in Right sector. The batteries of this Brigade were in readiness for counter battery work in accordance with our system of bombardment by the two Artillery Gp. but left beats of the enemy shind in the neighbourhood of PONT BALLOT salient. Nothing of interest. | H.A. B 36 No 1/2000 |
| | 17.2.16 | | A shoot was carried out against certain selected spots in the enemy front line and new. It is nothing in activity on the part of the enemy. It is reported that the large howe Battery to a Battery in our part of the line (by no of our F.O.Os) | H.A.B 36 No 1/2000 |
| | 18.2.16 | 11.30pm | Operations were carried out against front line and communication trenches in L'EPINETTE B. stock of 96 Brigades R.F.A was asked to be ready for counter battery work. The Brigade stood by for counter battery work, the Division being ordered to bombard the EPINETTE. No one was called upon to open fire. | Appendix B |
| | 19.2.16 | | The enemy however retaliated in our trenches by throwing during the whole day with a chief without for him, and heavily gun-fire largely called was bombarded against S19 and trenches did no damage. | +2's |
| | 20.2.16 | | Nothing of interest | |
| | 21.2.16 | | | |
| | 22.2.16 | | | |

**Army Form C. 2118.**

# WAR DIARY
## or
## INTELLIGENCE SUMMARY.

*(Erase heading not required.)*

at the Brigade Hrs. Sheet No. 25

Instructions regarding War Diaries and Intelligence Summaries are contained in F. S. Regs., Part II. and the Staff Manual respectively. Title pages will be prepared in manuscript.

| Place | Date | Hour | Summary of Events and Information | Remarks and references to Appendices |
|---|---|---|---|---|
| ♦ ♦ ♦ | 23.2.16 | | C/97 and A/96 had a small continued shoot against a house which was supposed to contain a gun. | |
| | 24.2.16 | | Another operation against enemy trench. Wire was cut for a distance of 20 yds. at I.11.a.4.3. Allotment of ammunition 120. Wire put 40 HE 3 L.N.W. The N/E. were reported to be quite visible for the air with the no. 5 gun 1/20,000. They accounted for the hard ground and burst in air. Orders were received for a bombardment of the enemy first line trenches from 10.30 to 11.30 p.m. Our infantry were ordered [illegible] at 11 p.m. The trench at I.5.d.1. to I.5.c.3. at 11 p.m. also, D/96 which was coming this part of the enemy trenches were ordered to gradually lift their fire. At 11.15 p.m. the order to stop fire was however given and we subsequently heard that the action was that the infantry had failed to face the German trenches. General Ferguson (the II Corps Commander) inspected the battery positions. orders have been received that we shall be relieving between the 1st and 10th March. | appendices |
| | 25.2.16 | | | |
| | 26.2.16 | | Nothing of special interest. | |
| | 27.2.16 | | | |
| | 28.2.16 | | | |
| | 29.2.16 | | | |

W. C. Coates, Maj. R.F.A.
Comdg. 96th Bde. R.F.A.

56 Bn C pr Oper Order N° 10 — A

The Right Section will bombard
sheet 20... square... Malines

A. Target 16pm 4/9/ in detail
    ...from... T to...
    ...batty has alone... ...centre
    Ammunition 30 rounds HE

B. Target 12.15pm. The 9 High... point... will be relieved
    of... ... batteries... ...
    ... HE ... ...
    at ... ... ... ...
    9. FERRET I-12 d 2.7.
    D/96 Road Junction and Track Tramway
        Terminus I 12 central
        Ammunition 10 rounds HE } pr Batty
                    50  "  Shrapnel

    +8  The enemy... as previous... be
        ... S/G ... new Front...

C. Communication Wire: A/96 ... B/96 according
    to instruction

D. Acknowledge.

Copy to A/96
        B/96
        C/96            Brig... Capt RFA
        O/96            Capt 26 Bde RFA
        C/97
        ...  ✓

Artillery Operation Order N° 1 — B

Artillery Operations will be carried out tomorrow 19th inst. as under.

1·20pm    C/97 will shell ARRÊT (I·12 central)
          LA FRESNETTE (I·12·b·2·5)
          Ammunition 36 rds HE
          fire will be deliberate
          Remaining Batteries of the Brigade
          will be ready for Counter Battery W...

... Batteries of the Divisional
Artillery will shell LE TEMPLE, L'AVENTURE
etc, also from our Trenches in their section.

It is possible that the Infantry may
for... Brigade...

D.    Acknowledge

Copies to
    A/32
    B/32
    C/32
    D/32
    C/97
    ...
                        Lt Col Cmdg RFA
                        Cmdg 26 Bde RFA

SECRET                                                                    C.

96 Bde Ord: Operation Order No 11.                              23-2-16

Reference: Trench Map.

1. A Minor Operation against the Enemy's Trenches as under will be carried out on Thursday 24th inst. The object of the Operation is to damage, destroy and capture Machine guns and Take some prisoners.

2. On Thursday 24th inst. commencing at 11am. C/97 will bombard the Railway Salient (I.11.a).
   At 12·30 pm. D/96 will cut the Enemy's Wire for a length of 30 yards at I.11.a.4.3.
   For Tasks see Table "A". (only sent to C/97 and D/96)

3. On Thursday 24th inst. The Enemy's Front Line, Support and Communication Trenches will be bombarded from 10·57pm to 11·30pm. At 11·0pm. fire will be lifted from the Front Trenches I.11.a.6.2 to I.5.d.0.5, but will continue on the Support and Communication Trenches to the East of them and on other points.
   At 11·0pm under cover of this fire, and of smoke bombs thrown into the Railway Salient, an Infantry Assault will be made on the Trenches from I.5.c.7.1 to I.5.c.8.3. The Infantry will retire to our lines by 11·30pm.
   For Tasks see Table "B".

4. After completion of Table "B" all Batteries will stand by in case of counter-attack.

5. Batteries will be ready to take on Counter Battery Work as detailed in Table C. (only sent to A/96, B/96, C/96 and C/97)

6. Reports during and on completion of Operation to be sent to this Office by Telephone.

7.   ACKNOWLEDGE.


Copies to A/96                                      B. Thelle Capt. RFA
         B/96                                       Adjt 96 Bde RFA.
         C/96
         D/96
         C/97.
         War Diary

Table "A"

| Unit | No. of guns. | Task | 18 Pdr. Shrap. H.E. | | 4.5 H.E. | Remarks |
|---|---|---|---|---|---|---|
| D/96 | 4 | Cut Wire at I.11.a.4.3. | 120 | 40 | | Commencing at 12:30 p.m. Rate of fire to be slow and deliberate. |
| C/97 | 4 | Bombard Railway Salient. | | | 20 | Commencing at 11:00 a.m. Rate of fire to be slow and deliberate. |

Table "B".  Bombardment and Assault.                                      Thursday Feby 24th 1916

| Unit | No of guns | Time From. P.M. | Time To. P.M. | Task | 18 Pdr. Shrap. | 18 Pdr. H.E. | H.E. | Remarks |
|---|---|---|---|---|---|---|---|---|
| B/96 | 2 | 10.57 | 11.0 | Front and Support Trenches. I.11.c.5½.3 to I.11.c.6.6 | 16 | 4 | | Section fire 10 secs. |
| | 2 | 11.0 | 11.30 | Barrage I.11.a.6½.9 to I.5.c.9.1. No rounds to fall North or West of this line | 90 | 50 | | Section fire 15 secs. |
| C/96 | 4 | 10.57 | 11.0 | Front and Support Trenches I.11.c.6.6 to I.11.a.5½.3 | 30 | 10 | | Section fire 15 secs. |
| | 4 | 11.0 | 11.30 | Ditto | 90 | 50 | | Section fire 30 secs. |
| | 4 | 10.57 | 11.0 | Front and Support Trenches. I.11.a.5½.3 to I.5.c.7.0 | 30 | 10 | | Section fire 10 secs. |
| D/96 | 2 | 11.0 | 11.30 | Barrage I.5.c.9.1 to I.5.d.1.2. No rounds to fall North or West of the line. | 90 | 50 | | Section fire 15 secs. |
| | 2 | 11.0 | 11.30 | Front and Support Trenches. I.11.a.5½.3 to I.11.a.6.7 | 90 | 50 | | The section employed for Barrage will lift its fire gradually. |
| C/97. | 4 | 10.57 | 11.30 | Bombard Railway Salient | | | 120 | |

N.B. Ammunition in all cases includes that necessary for Registration.

## Table "C"

| Battery at | Will be Engaged by |
|---|---|
| I.17.d.6.3 | A/96 and C/97. |
| I.30.a.2.7 | A/96 and C/97. |
| I.23.d.6.2 | B/96, C/96 and C/97. |
| I.18.a.2.2. | B/96, C/96 and C/97. |

21st Divisional Artillery.

----------

96th BRIGADE R. F. A.

MARCH 1916.

# WAR DIARY
## INTELLIGENCE SUMMARY

Army Form C. 2118.

Sheet No. 26

| Place | Date | Hour | Summary of Events and Information | Remarks and references to Appendices |
|---|---|---|---|---|
| ARMENTIERES | 1.3.16 | | Nothing to report | |
| | 2.3.16 | | | |
| | 3.3.16 | | Right relief carried out bombardment of the enemy's trenches lettered MUSHROOM I.11.c.3.4. (Sheet 36 N.W/20,000) with the object of obtaining the enemy guns. 300 rounds were fired from B/96 and A/96. Aim was fired up by number from C/96. We commenced at 1.30 P.M. and was replied by | Appended |
| | | 2.40 P.M. | C/96 (two) also took part as well as trench mortars. Range many 1PR No 150. Gaps were made and the parapet was badly damaged. Enemy trench guns fired on MUSHROOM and ARMENTIERES. We retaliated against enemy | |
| | 4.3.16 | 5 P.M. | The enemy put 50 rounds and 40 rounds per battery. The morning a tour of the district of our front line trenches was retaliated. | |
| | 5.3.16 | | Nothing distinct. There was a good many operations during the day. A certain amount of enemy trench was done. Also shelling of brick stack. A certain amount of shelter making parties had been aroused. Collections where in our positions underneath screening of guns. Purchased who passed on the ground of the faun patrolled opposite in the snows by the west of the | |
| | 6.3.16 | | | |
| | 7.3.16 | | | |
| | 8.3.16 | | | |
| | 9.3.16 | | | |
| | | | guns. | |
| | 12.3.16 | | Nothing of importance. | |
| | 13.3.16 | | Trench mortar fired on the railway culvert I.11.a.4.2. (36 N.W.). The drew a certain amount of retaliation into trenches. No enys. ammunition | |
| | 14.3.16 | | could hardly work help the Brigade. | |

# WAR DIARY
## or
## INTELLIGENCE SUMMARY

Army Form C. 2118.

(Erase heading not required.)

| Place | Date | Hour | Summary of Events and Information | Remarks and references to Appendices |
|---|---|---|---|---|
| ARMENTIERES | 9.3.16 | | 9/3/16 had men on working party erecting 2) PENTHES and mg stand nearer O.P. hange when have little taken by 4/1/3 Brigade and knew the latter having more to consolidate it & the Res Battery work. 96 Len used Raid now Z to ensuring of ty morning 10/3/16 Count Battery work. 96 Len used Raid Commanders of the batteries (Col CARDEW of the 11th) who am Batty Commander's had a meeting (afterwards call around to find the position. Following have been issued to afec — 3.3.16 3/5 Count run to find *LA KREVNE* on the following date window — Raft sample Sunday 13 Get on.<br>March 15th — 1 section A/96 and B/96<br>16th — A/96 and B/96 6th 1 section each<br>19th — 1 section C/96 and D/96<br>21st Am. Col.<br>22nd 1 section C/96 and D/96<br>23rd C/96 and D/96 6th 1 section each and Brigade H.Q. Pursue the usual month up to this ins and have had to dispense with shelters and equipment of this Bony. Consequent on issue & the reading the supply letting up pieces of metal with keep stuck by at trigger of each by reorders against the billeted batteries whatever has been installed for T.O.O. also all ita you can have company companies are accordance with II Corp & II (34/15) orders 1.3.16. | |
| | 10/6/16 2m | | The yearly stores go to Brigade R.F.A. arrived to take over Brigade H.g. for Lt-Hagan at 1.30 pm | |

Army Form C. 2118.

# WAR DIARY
## or
## INTELLIGENCE SUMMARY.
(Erase heading not required.)

Instructions regarding War Diaries and Intelligence Summaries are contained in F. S. Regs., Part ___ and the Staff Manual respectively. Title pages will be prepared in manuscript.

| Place | Date | Hour | Summary of Events and Information | Remarks and references to Appendices |
|---|---|---|---|---|
| ARMENTIERES | 17.3.16 | | 2/Lieut C.R.D. SCHAGEL R.F.A. "B" Battery who was wounded on 27-1-16 was struck off the strength previous their invalided to England (Authority:- 2nd Army R/A. 369. Dated 17.3.16) | |
| " | 18.3.16 | | 1 Sect. of A + B moved to rest area East of Hazebrouck on having over the wires for communications for 4 batteries from Div. at H.Q. through 96th Bde. Recce H.Qrs through Battle H.Q. a Bre. down to Batteries H.Q. and F.O.O.s + was estimated that 16 miles more load and wire was in use. and 25 miles more laid and under Battery arrangements. | |
| | 20.3.16 | | A + B Batteries (less one section) moved to rest area as above. | |
| | 21.3.16 | | Ammunition Column moved to rest area | |
| | 22.3.16 | | One section C + D Batteries moved to rest area | |
| | 23.3.16 | | C + D (less one section) + Bde H.Qrs moved to rest area Lt. R.L. NASH. left to take over duties of Adjt. of 97th Bde R.F.A. | |
| | 24.3.16 to 29.3.16 | | Rest. ↑ During this period G.O.C. The Army inspected B/96 and expressed himself as highly satisfied with the work done by the Brigade during the period. It was part of 7th Army arty at Armentières. | |

Army Form C. 2118.

# WAR DIARY

*or*

# INTELLIGENCE SUMMARY.

*(Erase heading not required.)*

August 29.

Instructions regarding War Diaries and Intelligence Summaries are contained in F. S. Regs., Part II. and the Staff Manual respectively. Title pages will be prepared in manuscript.

| Place | Date | Hour | Summary of Events and Information | Remarks and references to Appendices |
|---|---|---|---|---|
| Lahoussoye | 30.3.16 | | Advance party under Capt. Mills proceeded to 4th Army XIII Corps. at BUSSY headquarters. | |
| " | 31-3.16 | | H.Q. 96th Bde "A" Battery & 1/4 Amm Col. moved to new area by train the journey taking about 9 hours and a detour area at LONGUEAU. | |

#353 Wt. W2544/1454 700,000 5/15 D. D. & L. A.D.S.S./Forms/C. 2118.

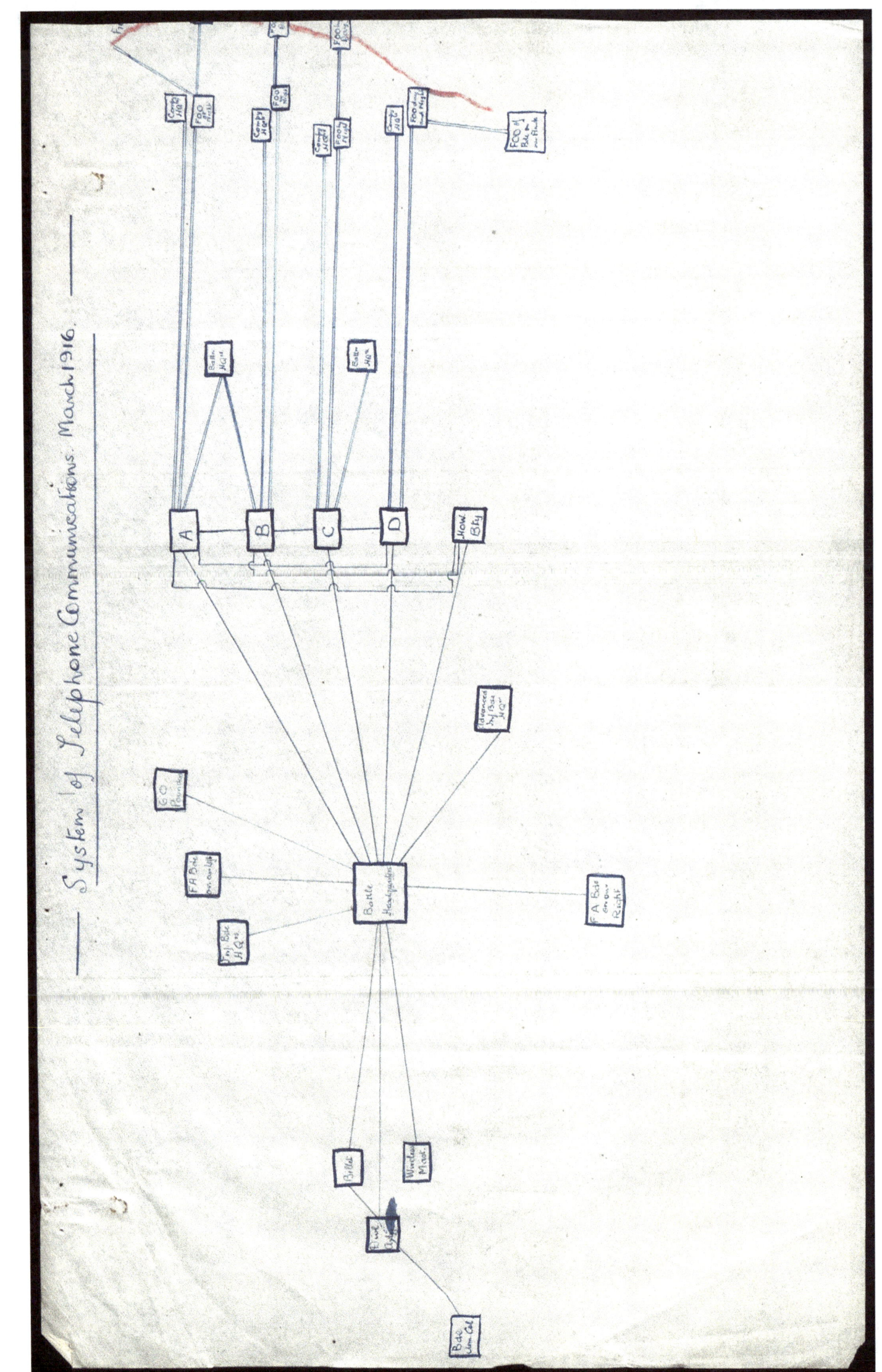

21st Divisional Artillery.

---------------

96th BRIGADE R. F. A.

A P R I L   1916.

96 RFA
Vol 8

Army Form C. 2118.

# WAR DIARY
## or
## INTELLIGENCE SUMMARY.
(Erase heading not required.)

Sheet 30.

| Place | Date | Hour | Summary of Events and Information | Remarks and references to Appendices |
|---|---|---|---|---|
| Bussy-les-Daours | 1-4-16 | | B C + D Batteries and Ammunition Col. (less 1/4) moved to new area billeting at (temporary) LONGUEAU. | |
| | 2-4-16 | | Rest | |
| | 4-4-16 | | Brigade Commander + Brigade Officers reconnoitred billeting position East of MEAULTE. | |
| | 5-4-16 | | Lt Col COATES ordered to England to Command A. Artillery 4th Division | |
| | 7-4-16 | | Lt Col. COATES left for England. Major COURTNEY temporarily in Command of the Brigade. | |
| | 9-4-16 | | Working parties from A + B batteries preparing the first to construct battery positions | |
| | 11-4-16 | | One section of C/96 went into action in position East of MEAULTE | |
| | 12-4-16 | | 1 O.R. B/96 wounded | |
| | 15-4-16 | | 1 O.R. A/96 wounded. Working parties from C + D batteries proceeded to the first to construct battery position. 1 O.R. C/96 wounded. | |
| | 16-4-16 | | Major COURTNEY apparative to the Command of the Brigade. | |
| | 23-4-16 | | A + B battery position under construction. Heavily shelled. No casualties | |
| | 26-4-16 | | Lieut R.B.WITHERS to 21st Heavy Siege Battery | |

F.J. Courtney
COL., R.F.A.
COMMANDING 96TH BRIGADE, R.F.A.

21st Divisional Artillery.
----------------

96th BRIGADE R. F. A.

M A Y  1916.

Army Form C. 2118.

**WAR DIARY or INTELLIGENCE SUMMARY.**

96th Bde R.F.A. Sheet 31.

No. 31  Date May /16

| Place | Date | Hour | Summary of Events and Information | Remarks and references to Appendices |
|---|---|---|---|---|
| BUSSY-LES-DAOURS | May 1st-3rd | | Nothing to report. | |
| | 4th | 10.30pm | Orders were received to move A & B Batteries into action on the positions they were building in F.4.C. (Sheet 62 DNE). On the 5th inst. D Battery and the remaining section of C Battery were to move up the following evening. O.C. C and D Batteries were not ready to occupy the positions of C Battery was ordered to occupy emplacements No.s F1.9.a. at BELLEVUE FARM (E.9.C.) and hence actually the IInd section of A{94}, D Battery will proceed to occupy one of the 18 french emplacements in F.9.b. The object of the move was merely for defensive purposes only in order to have one gun per 75 yards of line. These batteries were placed tactically under the 94th Brigade Group (Col Bannock) but remained for administrative purposes under O.C. 96th Brigade. | |
| BECORDEL | 5th | 9.30pm | A and B Batteries brought up the guns. While A Battery was crossing their guns into the emplacements the enemy put over about 30 4.2" and 5.9" shells in and round the position. No damage was done and the teams and the teams behaved splendidly in spite of the fact that one 5.9" shell fell between two teams. C and D Batteries moved up into action. Brigade Q recognition. Communications up to O.P.s. Bde Headquarters were temporarily established in Becourt 19 m E.12.b. | |
| do. | 6th | | | |
| do. | 7th | | A & B Batteries registered a few points in the enemy's lines. The enemy retaliated with a few rounds but no damage was done. | |
| do. | 8th | | C & D Batteries registered a few points. The R.Q.U section of C Battery (Bellevue Farm) was given a portion of the line to cover. A & B Batteries were ordered not to fire except in the case of a general attack, and the minimum amount of registration is to be done. | |
| do. | 9th-15th | | A & B Batteries were kept busy in improving their present positions and build their new positions while in action in the positions they went into on the 6th | |

# WAR DIARY or INTELLIGENCE SUMMARY

Army Form C. 2118.

(Erase heading not required.)

| Place | Date | Hour | Summary of Events and Information | Remarks and references to Appendices |
|---|---|---|---|---|
| BECORDEL | MAY 9-15 | | Orders had been issued that all guns & ammunition &c, &c/stores was to be stocked down below ioa[?] and a second entrance. Accommodation was to be made for 1,000 rounds per gun & a second entrance to each Gun Ranche dug to ensure the gun [?] and the dumps[?] till the entrance had been made without hindrance of any sort from the enemy. This was due mostly to the superiority of the R.F.C. as no German planes were allowed to cross our lines. This has been the case. | |
| " | 15th | | The Brigade Ammunition Column moved to about 3/4 mile of H.E. 3 Dugouts, now situated in the Divisional Column as the 3rd Section, H Echelon. San/ Col. Simultaneously Batt[?] & the RE dumps[?] was reorganised. C Battery was hence located at 92A Brigade and 146 c/37 (Howitzer By) became D/85 and D/15 in consequence became C/36 and HQs[?] in charge of 15 Inches Battery also 15cwt. F.A. Burnes 2 7 pdr. the Howitzer Battery | |
| " | 16-31st | | Nothing of importance occurred. The Battens[?] continued to improve their gun pits as were as the R.E. material was now available. Brigade HQ[?] moved into a dug out just [?] [?] and [?] on the south side of the ALBERT-FRICOURT Rd (E.12.2.3.8.) OC Brigade was hardly a moment disengaged [?] in the construction & one can OPs were selected and routes to positions fixed. The dugouts at 63 in the new harbour[?] around the track OPs were now finished at H.B.O.[?] having been found impractically toward old Grin trench 9x36: No. 3 dug out was not available. D3 had to be used, all that was needed on a dug out. During the month all OG wires and cable was changed. The systems is now in full operation and causes no worry. Advance [?] OPs were begun by R.E.RE in base supplies (F.2.6). On 28.3 FrH. wire entrance[?] had been completed but no actual excavations of the dug outs had been begun. The Sanitary arrangements were greatly improved during the month. All latrines were dug 6 feet deep and 18 inches broad. The 3rd was rendered flyproof. Fly seat[?] being provided with a tightly fitting cover. During [?] the fly nuisance and Epidemic became and [?] now the weather became warmer. | |

96 RFA
Vol 9

Army Form C. 2118.

XXI

## WAR DIARY
## or
## INTELLIGENCE SUMMARY.

Sheet 33

(Erase heading not required.)

Instructions regarding War Diaries and Intelligence Summaries are contained in F. S. Regs., Part II. and the Staff Manual respectively. Title pages will be prepared in manuscript.

| Place | Date | Hour | Summary of Events and Information | Remarks and references to Appendices |
|---|---|---|---|---|
| BECOURDEL | 1/6 - 31/5 | | Two Junior Officers (Lt Campbell and 2/Lt Sandford) attended the 4th Army School of Instruction at MAVERNAS during the month. Major Horning and Sandford also attended a course in Trench Mortars at the School near AMIENS | |
| | 3-6-16 | | | |

TH Partley Lieut Col. RFA
Commanding 96th Bde R.F.A.

[Stamp: 96th BRIGADE No 33 Date May 1916 R.F.A.]

21st Divisional Artillery.
-------------------------------

96th BRIGADE R. F. A.

J U N E  1916.

Army Form C. 2118.

June/July

Vol 10

# WAR DIARY
or
## INTELLIGENCE SUMMARY.

(Erase heading not required.)

Sheet 34.

| Place | Date | Hour | Summary of Events and Information | Remarks and references to Appendices |
|---|---|---|---|---|
| BECORDEL | 1.6.16 to 23.6.16 | | Bde HdQrs. & Batteries continued to occupy the same positions as last month. During the period 16/19. The following batteries moved into their new positions, C/96 to D/96 to F.17.d.9.9. They were relieved by two batteries of the 79th Bde R.F.A. 17th Division under the C.O. R.F. Castle. A new position at F.2.a.6.4 was selected for Howitzer battery of the 79th Bde & taken over & completed by them from 17.F.inct. All battery positions were filled with 400 rds. a over during the period 6.s/6. 23.6.16. Ammunition was supplied by lorries & carted from near to battery positions by hand. The Vacaville Railway was completed from ALBERT to BECORD WOOD & is to be used for supplying various batteries with returns & ammunition, among which are A/96, B/96, D/96. On 21.6.16 a camouflage Trench O.P. was drawn from AMIENS & placed in position near AVERLY by A/96. 2nd A.C. GREEN on promotion from X Battery R.H.A. was posted to A/96. During this period 2nd Lt. SANFORD attended a course of Heavy Trench Mortars & returned to his battery on 19/6/16. | |
| | 19.6.16 | | | |

Army Form C. 2118.

# WAR DIARY
or
## INTELLIGENCE SUMMARY.

Sheet 35

(Erase heading not required.)

| Place | Date | Hour | Summary of Events and Information | Remarks and references to Appendices |
|---|---|---|---|---|

2/Lt. HORNING was posted to the Medium Trench Mortar Bn. L.R. Morzed

Struck off the strength of the Bde from that date.

95th Bde Hqs. moved up to Rear battle HQ at junction of SHUTTLE LANE & 101 STREET on evening of 23.6.18.

The following Officers & men received awards in the June Despatch.

Military Cross.    Capt. A. S. J. PARK.

Mentioned in } Capt. N. M. McLEOD, 2 Lt. H. D. BRYDONE-JACK,
Despatches  } No 35147 Sgt. E. C. F. DUNSTAN & No 13795 Gr. D. E. WILSON.


J. McInkay Lt. Col. R.F.A.
Comdg 96th Bde R.F.A.

Army Form C. 2118.

# WAR DIARY
## or
## INTELLIGENCE SUMMARY.
(Erase heading not required.)

96th Bde R.F.A.      Sheet 36.

| Place | Date | Hour | Summary of Events and Information | Remarks and references to Appendices |
|---|---|---|---|---|
| BECORDEL | 24th July 16 | 11.30 am | Commencement of wire cutting & bombardment per 4th Army front commenced. | A.1.15* |
| | | | Batteries of Brigade cut wire as shown in attached appendix. Table "A" sheet. | A.2 |
| | 25th & 26th | | Night bombardment as shown in Table "B". Wire cutting continued. Results excellent. | |
| | 26th | 3:30 p | Bombardment as per Table "C". At 9 am gas was discharged from our front trenches also smoke. | A.3 |
| | 27th | | Bombardment as per Table "D". | A.4 |
| | 28th | | Bombardment as per Table "E". Assault postponed 48 hrs. Lt. Col. Gouley & Lt. King wounded. | A.5 |
| | 29th | | do "A" | A.1 |
| | 30th | | do "B" | A.2 |
| | 31st | | do "C" | A.3 |
| | 1st | 6:15 am | Bombardment as per appendix attached, commenced. Table "H". | A.6 |
| | | 7:30 am | Batteries lifted on to lines shown in Table "H" | } do |
| | | 7.47 | do | |
| | | 8.15 | do | |
| | | 8.45 | do | |
| | | 9.55 | do | |
| | | about 10 am | do Flt 63 hy. bde. had been unable to advance father than LOZENGE |  |

War Diary

DM.100

INSTRUCTIONS FOR OFFENCE NO 4.

- BARRAGES -

1. On "Z" day a concentrated bombardment will be carried out starting 65 minutes before zero. Zero will be the time at which the assault commences.

2. The advance of the Infantry will be prepared and covered by bombardments and barrages until the final objective is reached.

   The different phases of the bombardments and times for Divisional Artilleries are shewn in Table "G". Table "H" shows tasks allotted to Brigades R.F.A. Tracings "C","D", "E", "F", "G", "H" & "K", show the distribution of fire of batteries at each bombardment.

3. After the final objective has been reached, there will be a bombardment of the FRICOURT area. A special zero time for the attack on FRICOURT will be arranged and the bombardment will start 30 minutes before that zero time. Table "K" shows tasks and times for the special bombardment. Table "L" and Tracings "L", "M" & "N" shows allotment of these tasks to Brigades.

4. With regard to Barrages. Attention is called to the following points:-

   (a) It is necessary to bring a heavy fire to bear on the part to be attacked immediately.

   (b) Objectives in rear should be treated at the same time but with less heavy fire.

   (c) All fire should be searching in nature, guns should be told off to search communication trenches &c.

   (d) When lifting, 18-pounder batteries will search back by increasing their range gradually, but howitzers will lift directly on to their next objective.

   (e) When barraging open ground, fire should be in bursts, searching back as far as necessary and not at a continuous rate. Woods and hollows beyond the actual line laid down should be searched.

5. The area not immediately to be attacked (FRICOURT area) must be kept under fire.

6. All the guns and trench mortars of divisional artillery will be employed for the above purposes.

7. Divisional Artillery H.Q. will be in touch with 1 Siege Artillery Group and 1 Heavy Artillery Group, so that the assistance of a small number of Siege Howitzers or Guns may be available. Brigade Commanders in forwarding applications for special treatment of any particular point, must ensure that all available information concerning exact locality etc., is forwarded with the application.

2.

8. On "Z" day all Battery Commanders should be in their O.P's.

9. A Battery Commander should be given a free hand to open fire without delay on any point which is holding up our Infantry, if he considers that the situation demands it.

If his battery is already firing according to the programme, a Battery Commander must be prepared to justify his reasons for changing on to a new objective.

It is impossible to enumerate all the reasons which would justify his doing so, but a counter-attack by the enemy might be an example.

10. A continuous fire should never be ordered, but a definite and limited number of rounds should always be stated. If no further order is received, then the allotted task according to Programme should be resumed by the Battery. This is most important, in case the wire between the O.P. and Battery should be cut.

11. If he considers that the fire of his own battery is not sufficient to deal with the situation, then he should report to his Brigade Commander what he considers necessary. For instance, a Strong Work will require to be dealt with by Heavy Howitzers.

12. A Battery Commander should go forward after the Infantry attack, when it is reasonably safe for him to do so, and when he will be able to see the situation better by advancing. He must not, however, lose touch with his Battery and his Brigade Commander.

To enable him to carry out these duties, he will require plenty of wire, two or more telephones, and at least three telephonists. These men should be armed with rifles, and be provided with two days' Rations.

R. Wellesley.
Brigadier-General. R.A.
18th June 1916.   Commanding, 21st Divisional Artillery.

War Diary Copy.

## TABLE "L" - FRICOURT ATTACK.

- Special Zero Time -

| TIME FROM TO | UNIT | TASK |
|---|---|---|
| -0.30  0.0 | 1 Bty 78 Bde | F.9.b.4.5. to F.3.d.1005: Front & Support. |
|  | 2 "    " | Area F.3.d.7.2. to F.3.d.9.7.to F.4.a.2560 to F.4.c.2046 |
|  | 1 "  97 Bde | Front & Support F.3.d.1005 to F.3.c.8.5. |
|  | 1 "  94 " | F.3.c.8.5.to F.3.c.6.9. to F.3.d.6.8. to F.3.d.5015 |
|  | 1 "C 96 " | F.4.a.0.0.to F.4.a.2560 to F.4.a.9585 to F.4.b.0.5. |
|  | 2 "  94 Group | X.27.d.6.1. to X.28.c.0045 to X.28.c.9515 to F.4.a.3.6. |
|  | D/94 | FRICOURT WOOD, West of Line F.4.b.0.5 to F.4.b.0.8. |
|  | D/79 | FRICOURT VILLAGE South of Line F.3.c.6.8. to F.3.d.6.8. |
| 0.0  0.15 | 1 Bty,78 Bde & D/79 | Area F.3.d.9.9.to F.3.b.7520 to F.3.b.9.8. to F.4.a.8.5. |
|  | 1 C Bty,96 Bde & D/94 | Area F.3.b.9.8.to F.4.b.0085 to F.4.b.2.7. to F.4.a.8.5. |
| 0.15  0.30 | 1 Bty,78 Bde & D/79 | Area F.4.a.2005 to F.3.b.9.6.to F.4.a.0280 to F.4.a.4580 to F.4.a.6535. |
|  | 1 C Bty,96 Bde & D/94 | Area F.4.a.6535 to F.4.a.4580 to X.28.c.9815 to F.4.b.2.7. |

AMMUNITION:  18-pounders, 26 (36) rounds a gun Shrapnel.
                         40  "     "   "   H. E.
             4.5 Howitzers, 40 (85) rounds a gun.

| | TRENCH MORTARS | |
|---|---|---|
| -0.30  0.0 | Heavy Mortars | F.3.d.1.1.     3 rounds. F.3.c.6936      3  " |
| "    " | Medium  " | F.9.b.0275    12  " German TAMBOUR 12  " |

21st Divisional Artillery.

----------------

96th BRIGADE R. F. A.

J U L Y  1916.

# WAR DIARY
## or
## INTELLIGENCE SUMMARY.

*(Erase heading not required.)*

Army Form C. 2118.

Sheet 37

| Place | Date | Hour | Summary of Events and Information | Remarks and references to Appendices |
|---|---|---|---|---|
| | | | ALLEY & EMPRESS SUPPORT the line of the Bn. was brought near to the LONELY TRENCH, FRICOURT FARM, THE POODLES, CRUCIFIX & BRIGHT TRENCH while preparatory & held the northern edge of FRICOURT & FRICOURT WOOD. During the night the Bde. Harassed the land x roads & front with M.G. & rifle fire in front of our infantry. About 11 pm the infantry sent up an S.O.S. signal from the SOUTHERN way of LOZENGE WOOD to the enemy wire counter attacking from NORTH of TRENCH & RED LANE. As arrangements had been made to meet such an attack the batteries of the Bde. opened fire put up a barrage in front of the trench held by our infantry in a few seconds, killing all the enemy who were left. Few trenches & prisoners taken from pillbox. The Bde. received the second tranch of its G.O.R. 63" Hy. Hut. 92 Return was hitted in the morning while another in wounded when from NO MANS LAND. | |
| | | | The southern end of FRICOURT WOOD noted in 2nd ... and was our collection FRICOURT VILLAGE & WOOD had been evacuated by the enemy during the night. The 17th DIVISION attacked them before them set out & proper fire. | |

# WAR DIARY or INTELLIGENCE SUMMARY

Army Form C. 2118.

Sheet 38.

| Place | Date | Hour | Summary of Events and Information | Remarks and references to Appendices |
|---|---|---|---|---|
| | | | Much valuable information was sent in by the Battery F.O.O.'s it was probably due to their observation that the F.O.C. 63rd Bde & consed alter the 21st Div. & 15th Corps knew when the 63rd infantry were in what was retiring. The F.O.E. of this brigade was lifted in confirmation with the infantry's advance ultimately. By the enemy the Battery FOO's were able to telephone to the infantry and indeed found that in order to see any thing they had to advance with them. By this time our infantry were in possession of the following, PRICOURT FARM, CRUCIFIX, CRUCIFIX TRENCH. During the night of the 2/3 the Bde hanged on the line X28a 3.9 To X28a 45.70 To X2.28 b.25.45. | B1 |
| | 3rd | 9.40 a.m | To assist our infantry to advance & capture SHELTER & BIRCH TRENCH WOODS an intense bombardment was ordered, during which the Bde shelled SHELTER WOOD RIFLE D/96 whilst 2 batteries of 118 Bde. searched its hedge between SHELTER & BOTTOM WOOD. During the morning at AMOROSO 20/06 hours killed while assisting the infantry he left his a large party of Fritzs away who were in RAILWAY ALLEY. During the day the Bde was employed in supporting the infantry who were engaged in ??? the 21st Div. infantry and during the night 3/4 the 21st Div. infantry had ??? but the 21st DA remained in the line. | C1 D1 |

# WAR DIARY
## or
## INTELLIGENCE SUMMARY. Sheet 39

Army Form C. 2118.

| Place | Date | Hour | Summary of Events and Information | Remarks and references to Appendices |
|---|---|---|---|---|
| | 3rd | | During the day W3d to W3a inclusive communication trenches N.T.E. & Reach were very intermittently shelled with 4.2" & 5.9" H.E. by 21st D.A. | E.1 |
| | 4th | | During the day the Bn's shelled various points in front. Between the squares a demonstration was being made that the Bde was to attack. Advance from positions near BOTTOM's SWEEP towards MUNSTER. Advance from positions BA5d X22d, x22b, x16a1. VILLA, M.O. squares by Left of Bde TRENCH TRAVERSE EUSTON x5.10 c.1. View nothing was observed out of ordinary except enemy aeroplanes over LINES. ACID DROP COPSE up to 12 noon light Two 18pr batteries of Div. Art'y supported the Infantry advance of Inf Bde 3rd. | E.1 |
| | 5th | 12 noon | X2Rd 8.6.6. x22 6.5.2, x22a1. 48.3 x22a1 7. at 12.45am the batteries first opened to the barrage X23a 77.6, x17g.5.1.8 x17.c2.0 while H.E. how battery barraged ACID DROP COPSE & CONTALMAISON CEMETERY. 12.01 to 12.15am the 18pdrs kept up a slow rate of fire on ACID DROP COPSE from 12.45am to 1.15am QUADRANGLE TRENCH having been taken by the infantry, firing ceased. The whole day consolidation was carried by the few of morning 18pdrs was made along the Bde front Priority to enemy wire supplied by the battery H.D.O.S. + the Hy during the day counter-fired to a considerable number, mostly in + around CONTALMAISON. Later in the day the Bde barraged QUADRANGLE SUPPORT & PEARL ALLEY. During the day fire was on trenches on front same line 70th Inf Bde H/Qrs Y/QDts Hrs | E.1 |
| | | 2.45am | | G.1 |

Army Form C. 2118.

# WAR DIARY
or
## INTELLIGENCE SUMMARY. Sheet 4D.
(Erase heading not required.)

| Place | Date | Hour | Summary of Events and Information | Remarks and references to Appendices |
|---|---|---|---|---|
| | 6th | | A day similar to the 5th inst | |
| | 7th | 1.25 am | Bde bombed QUADRANGLE SUPPORT & QUADRANGLE ALLEY 52nd Bde seen when 52 Bde attacked PEARL ALLEY, QUADRANGLE SUPPORT + ALLEY. On 18 pr Battery remained engaged on + southern edges of CONTALMAISON. | H.1 |
| | | 2 am | Bde barraged EASTERN SOUTHERN edges of CONTALMAISON. 2.30 am in the pm was turned on to wooded night lines during the day various fleeting targets engaged | |
| | | 7.30 am | Bombardment of WOOD X23d 5.8 to X23d 4.7 with 3 Battery 13pm & [?] & also HOWN WOOD SUPPORT | H.2 |
| | | 8 am | Infantry attacked QUADRANGLE SUPPORT ACID DROP COPSE + WOOD between WOOD TRENCH + WOOD SUPPORT Batteries lifted to cum moves at X 24 a 8.9. Local night firing 7.30 place after works. | |
| | 8th | 7.30 am | Bde bombarded X17d 85.70 to X18a 55.4 to X18a 90.55 7 X 18a 23 to X17a 85.70. | I.1 |
| | | 8 am | Batteries lifted back into the WOOD N of the line S.19 central to X24a 65.30 to X17a 7.4 whilst infantry of 17th + 38th Divisions attacked wood. | |
| | | 8.30 am | Fire lifted North of line East + West through X18c central S.13 central | |
| | | 9 am | do do | |
| | | 9.30 am | fire lifted to North of MAMETZ WOOD | |
| | | | During the day an infantry news driven out of QUADRANGLE SUPPORT and bttering were used as on previous days. | |

# WAR DIARY
## or
## INTELLIGENCE SUMMARY.

*(Erase heading not required.)*

Army Form C. 2118.

Instructions regarding War Diaries and Intelligence Summaries are contained in F.S. Regs., Part II. and the Staff Manual respectively. Title pages will be prepared in manuscript.

| Place | Date | Hour | Summary of Events and Information | Remarks and references to Appendices |
|---|---|---|---|---|
| | 3/2 | 5.25am | Bombardment string of WMP from x.13 - s.18 & x.23 se & y - WOOD SUPPORT. | J.1 |
| | | 5.30am | Infantry attacked 500 yards ahead of QUADRANGLE SUPPORT. Front line + PEARL ALLEY & junction of QUADRANGLE ALLEY & SUPPORT | |
| | | 6.30pm | Barrage beyond line front | |
| | | | Remainder of day as usual. Our infantry unable to break shoulder to meeting | |
| | | | afternoon. Night times too short | |
| | 9/2 | | Usual amount of work any heavy target presenting itself on mark | K.1 |
| | | 11.0pm | Our infantry again attacked QUADRANGLE SUPPORT, 7th R. [?] 36th Bn | |
| | | 11.30pm | Barrage from 11.30pm to 12.0pm on WOOD SUPPORT & PEARL ALLEY & line beyond at night at intervals | |
| | 10/2 | 3.30am | 2/4 Bns of 2nd Division attacked WOOD from X.23 a.1.9 to X.23.25.8 two coys in | L.1 |
| | | | 2 companies | |
| | | 4am | Gun fires on front edge of WOOD | |
| | | 4.15 | Slow hostile [?] [?] back [?] minutes only | |
| | | 6.15 | Barrage back to S14 & S15.35. Or x.24.6.35 to WOOD SUPPORT to X.23.b.25 & line S13.d. to X to N VIRG.5.20 to X.28.b.9.5 | |
| | | 7.15am | All from S. reached back to N.W. edge of WOOD | |
| | | 8am | All from Pearl Lane to GERMAN ALLEY & hang out | |

Army Form C. 2118.

# WAR DIARY
## or
## INTELLIGENCE SUMMARY.  Sheet 42.
(Erase heading not required.)

| Place | Date | Hour | Summary of Events and Information | Remarks and references to Appendices |
|---|---|---|---|---|
| | 10th | 3.30 | Bombardment Sups of W.O.T.D x23c 3.0 to x23a 4.6 LOST COPSE & WOOD SUPPORT. | L1 |
| | | 4.15am | Bombarded rest to x23b.5.8 to x18 a.2.0 | |
| | | 7.15am | Searched rest to x18.a.2.3 to 8.13.a.2.2 | |
| | | 8.15a | Searched back in direction 2nd LINE to band of 18pr range when 18 hrs searched 2nd LINE between x12&7 to 8.7 a. 2.0. hour) D/96 Howitzer 2nd LINE between x12&7 to 8.7a.2.0 During remainder of day + night brigade arranged to bombard + harassed - front of no mans land. Later bombardment Infantry arranged. Orders received for bombardment of 2nd LINE commencing on 11th inst next. was postponed 24 hours. | |
| MAMETZ | 11th | | Orders received to move up two 18pr batteries to new positions in x29d. A Battery was able to get into position but B Battery had to go back to their old position again. A Battery started wire cutting on Bde. Zone viz 8.14.a.7.3 to 8.14.a.1.6 | M1 |
| | 12th | | remaining 18 pr battery moved up during the night to new positions in x29d. while A Battery crossed to Bde zone in s.14.a. N.A.2.96th Bde. arrived up to main zone position in VALLEY TRENCH (x29d.0.3.) The Howitzer battery also moved up during the night to valley E of BOTTOM WOOD) | N1 |
| | 13th | | Wire cutting carried out TD whole day in 3rd LINE S.14.a.7.3 to S.14.2.1.6 by the three 8pr batteries while the Hour. Battery bombarded the front + supplementary behind Bde zone. During the night 13/14 of [crossed out] batteries bombarded x-roads, support lines to prevent reinforcements being long up |

Army Form C. 2118.

# WAR DIARY
## or
## INTELLIGENCE SUMMARY.

*(Erase heading not required.)*

Instructions regarding War Diaries and Intelligence Summaries are contained in F.S. Regs., Part II. and the Staff Manual respectively. Title pages will be prepared in manuscript.

| Place | Date | Hour | Summary of Events and Information | Remarks and references to Appendices |
|---|---|---|---|---|
| | 14R | 3.22am | All batteries bombarded front & support trenches & approx's known as Bde Front in S.14.a.1.6. | O₁ |
| | | 3.3am | Howitzers sounded back gradually to German 3rd line as attack reached RED LINE | |
| | | | 18 pr batteries do | BLUE LINE |
| | | 3.30am | do | RED LINE |
| | | 4.20am | Howitzers | YELLOW LINE |
| | | 4.24am | 18 pr batteries do | do |
| | | 5.20am | Howitzers do | do |
| | | 5.25am | 18 pr batteries do | do |
| | | 5am | Howitzers | GREEN LINE |
| | | 5.45am | 18 pr batteries do | do |
| | | 6am | Howitzers do | PURPLE LINE |
| | | 6.50am | 18 pr batteries do | do |
| | | 6.30am | Howitzers searched back to several M.G. STATIONS – LES PETIT x other villages | BROWN LINE |
| | | 6.30am | 18 pr batteries searched back to the German 2nd & 3rd line. Maintained front of the village. During the day various points were shelled – a steady fire was kept up from the SWITCH TRENCH in S.8a & @ M.32. Barrages for night reverse as for day. All rounds to Poelcapelle were kept under fire. | P₁ |

# WAR DIARY or INTELLIGENCE SUMMARY

Army Form C. 2118.

Sheet A4.

| Place | Date | Hour | Summary of Events and Information | Remarks and references to Appendices |
|---|---|---|---|---|
| | 15th | | In progress of recent Infantry advanced to 2.Bta. HIGH WOOD not now occupied at night. They also cleared up BAZENTIN-LE-PETIT-LEGRAND FTZ Villages + woods + consolidated themselves in their new front. Hostile counter attacks were repulsed by artillery fire. What's front of SWITCH TRENCH in M33c was cut + remainder of trench in Bazn. from M2 Report Machine gun during day + night. | Q1 Q2 Q3 |
| | 16th | 8.30am | Bombardment of SWITCH TRENCH from M33c02 to B.26.3580 | |
| | | 9am | 18pdrs searched back + howitzers by A.F.A. to MARTIN PUICH & the area enclosed by M32cta. The Infantry assault was not successful + fire for rest of the day + night was kept up on SWITCH TRENCH + country beyond, as shown in SKETCH. HIGH WOOD was evacuated by 7th Division early in the morning. During the night A.B + C Batteries 91st Bde R.F.A. moved up to new position near FLATIRON COPSE (S14c) Head Quarters did not move. | |
| BAZENTIN LE-PETIT | 17th | | Batteries of the Bde registered from new position + cut wire in M33c etc. They also bombarded portion of SWITCH TRENCH in their front + country beyond. During the day the three 18pdr batteries were heavily shelled by 5.9"s. Two guns of A battery were knocked out + H.D.R. killed + 23 wounded. In various times the positions had to be evacuated but night firing was carried out on SWITCH TRENCH + country beyond | |

# WAR DIARY or INTELLIGENCE SUMMARY

Army Form C. 2118.

Sheet No 5

| Place | Date | Hour | Summary of Events and Information | Remarks and references to Appendices |
|---|---|---|---|---|
| | 18th | | During the day usual firing in both zones. 18 hr. Battery shelled A/96 moved its position to high ground E of FLATIRON COPSE & B/96 had about 200 x light firing but were likely at addition M33c (S.30pm) to M33c + 50 yds MARTIN was intended at 3.30am. | R |
| | 19th | | Usual firing in SWITCH TRENCH by day also normal activity by night. Hay/dump at M33c.00 to M33e.71.3. Division A/96 kept MARTIN PUICH under fire. | S |
| | 20th | 2.55am | Bombarded SWITCH TRENCH (M33c.00 to M33d.15.30) with 18pr. Shrapnel. Howitzers bombarded Same line M33c. 25.20 to M33c.61 | |
| | | 4.30am | 18 pr. South B line M34b.00 to M33d.ST.01. 2H Amphios B/96 who had been sent forward to strong point in S19 Central was unable to use the phone, at 3.25am XV Corps ordered SWITCH TRENCH to but were repulsed. During the day the unused firing in SWITCH TRENCH to passages + night firing carried out, a SWITCH TRENCH from M33.d.00 to M33.d.93. Howitzers on S.24.46 & M33 c.3.2 & occasional bursts of fire on MARTIN PUICH. Howitzers using 8.K. shells. | W |
| | 21st | | The day + night passed as usual. Firing carried out on zones as by day + night. | |
| | 22nd | 3.10am | Concentrated bombardment on M33d.6500 M35d.25.15 A.30am with 18 pr. shrapnel that 300 yds. | X |
| | | 3.30am | Howitzers ceased firing while 18 pr. searched that 300 yds extra before advancing night firing was otherwise as usual. | |

| Place | Date | Hour | Summary of Events and Information | Remarks and references to Appendices |
|---|---|---|---|---|
| | 22nd | 7pm | Bombarded SWITCH TRENCH 20 pdrs. 18 pr batteries S.34.0.7. S.34.90.95's Howitzers S.36.90.75. M.33.d.5.1. 18 pr batteries searched ground up to 3 ozpes S. + 2n yds N y TRENCH Swing ten | Y.1 |
| | 23rd | 1.27am | Howitzers bombarded trenches A.13.d.9.9. + then opened firing 18 pr batteries searched land to Long A.13.12. 200 yds N. of this continued to search ground beyond T. 300.400 yds. Infantry assailed trench at 1.30am but were repulsed | |
| | | 1.30am | During the day + night unused fire on Balc. 30M. Night fire S.4.a.76 to S.+Z.4.5. Used fire by Coys on B26 gun at 11 am. B26 started to withdraw to BONNAY on being relieved by 51st DIVISIONAL ARTILLERY. Batteries marching independently | Z.1 |
| BONNAY | 24th | 7pm | Last battery arrived at BONNAY.<br>Casualties during period 24.6.16 to 24.7.16 as follows:<br>Killed officers O.R.<br>2nd Lieut. Adamu 10. Wounded officers O.R.<br>" ammn. Lt.Col Crichley 43<br>Lt. King<br>2/Lt. Campbell<br>Lt. OSBORNE<br>2/Lt. Begg<br>" Busby<br>" Trottel<br>" Mahgim<br>Capt. Stenhouse RAMC<br>Of these Lt. Fitzhenry<br>were telegraphed as dead<br>men.<br>Killed 19 men died<br>4 14 | |

Army Form C. 2118.

# WAR DIARY
## *or*
## INTELLIGENCE SUMMARY.
(Erase heading not required.)

Instructions regarding War Diaries and Intelligence
Summaries are contained in F. S. Regs. Part II.
and the Staff Manual respectively. Title pages
will be prepared in manuscript.

| Place | Date | Hour | Summary of Events and Information | Remarks and references to Appendices |
|---|---|---|---|---|
| | 24/5 | | Total number of rounds fired during this period of days battery ned 1357. | |
| | | | | 24 Infantry 4 Coy |
| | 7.5.16. | | | bn o/g 90 8 Feb R.F.A |

### 96th Bde. Operation Order No 1.    A    16-6-16

1. The XV Corps has been ordered to attack with the line S.2.S.6.58.32 - X.29.b.5.6 - X.22.b.6.8 as its ultimate objective.

   The 21st Division will attack with the 63rd Infantry Brigade on the right, and the 64th Infantry Brigade on the left. The 62nd Infantry Brigade will be in Divisional Reserve.

2. A preliminary bombardment will be carried out on "U", "V", "W", "X" and "Y" days. Wire will be cut during all five days.

   On "V", "W", "X" and "Y" days and during the nights U/V and Y/Z inclusive, a continuous bombardment will be carried out.

   On "V" & "W" days there will be one, and on "X" & "Y" days two concentrated bombardments.

   Gas will be discharged on the first night the wind is favourable, and smoke on the morning of "X" day if direction of wind permits.

3. The attack will be launched at Zero on "Z" day.

4. Batteries will be grouped and located as follows:-

   A/96 at F.1.c.2.3
   B/96 at F.1.c.4.6.
   C/96 at F.7.b.4.1.
   D/96 at X.25.d.8.0.
   HQrs with 63rd Inf. Bde at F.2.b.7.9.
   HQrs 21st Divl Arty with HQrs 21st Div. at E.28.a.3.4

5. Zones: Dividing Line between 94th & 96th Brigades:

   X.27.c.40.15. - X.28.c.2.9 (FRICOURT FARM inclusive to 94th Bde) - X.28.b.3.1 (RAILWAY COPSE inclusive to 94th Bde) - X.23.d.4.0.

   Dividing Line between 96th & 97th Brigades:

   X.26.d.8.7. - X.28.b.0.8 - X.23.d.3.7 (LOZENGE WOOD inclusive to 96th Bde)

6. Wire Cutting: (a) On "U" day the wire in front of the Front Line will be cut by Medium Trench Mortars. 18 Pdr Batteries will commence by cutting the wire in front of the SUNKEN ROAD, and will continue with tasks in the order shown in Table "A" and Sketch "A".

   The remaining wire in front of the Front Line will be dealt with not later than the morning of "V" day.

   (b) On "U" day there will be no limit to expenditure of Ammunition on Wire Cutting.

   On "V", "W", "X" & "Y" days, 100 rounds per gun may be expended on Wire Cutting. During these days every opportunity of cessation of fire of Heavy Howitzers should be taken to carry on with the Wire Cutting. This however may be altered at the discretion of the Brigade Commander.

2

7. **Preliminary Bombardment:** (a) The tasks for the preliminary bombardment, commencing on the night of V day, and continuing on V, W, X, Y and Z days, are laid down in Tables B, C, D & E.

(b) The tasks are numbered and the times at which they are carried out will be issued each day.

(c) There will be special concentrated bombardments as under:—

   V day    4.0 p.m. to 6.0 p.m.
   W day    9.0 a.m. to 10.30 a.m.
   X day    4.0 a.m. to 5.00 a.m.
   Y day    6.30 p.m. to 7.0 a.m.
            6 a.m. to 7 a.m.
            4.0 p.m. to 5.30 p.m.

(d) The gas and smoke discharges will be accompanied by a heavy shrapnel barrage on the front line trenches and enemy's Communication Trenches.

8. **Barrage:** Immediately previous to the assault, an Artillery Barrage will be concentrated on the hostile front and close support trenches. As the attack progresses this barrage will lift.

The lift will be carried out at the hours named.

In lifting their fire, Batteries will search back to the next barrage, in order that the whole of ground may be covered by fire immediately before our Infantry advance over it.

Batteries not required for the Main Barrage will open fire at a slower rate of fire on portions of the subsequent lift.

Table of Barrages will be issued later.

9. **Liaison Officer:** The O.C. of Battery will be with the O.C. 95th S.I. Bde. When 95th Bde. H.Q. moves forward the Liaison Officer will move forward with them. He will establish telephone communication with O.C. Bde. and it will be his duty to send back information to O.C. Bde.

10. **Movement of Batteries:** On Z day, teams of all Batteries and DAC will be harnessed up and stand by, ready to move at short notice.

11. Battery Commanders will see that the tasks of their personnel are so arranged that each man gets as much rest as possible.

12. A reserve of 3 days rations, in addition to the iron ration and ordinary supply, will be arranged at each Battery Position.

Arrangements will also be made for a supply of drinking water.


Copies to   A/96.
            B/96.
            C/96.
            D/96.
            War Diary.

                                    B.M. & Capt. R.F.A.
                                    Adjt. 96 Bde. R.F.A.

## 96th Brigade Operation Orders No 1. (continued).

13. From night of "U"/"V" to night "Y"/"Z" both inclusive there will be pauses in the bombardment, to allow Infantry Patrols to go out to examine enemy wire. Time of pauses will be notified later.

14. If a re-bombardment of any point is ordered, a time for starting will be fixed and the bombardment will always last for half an hour from that time.

   The last five minutes should be intense so that the infantry may have warning.

   This would also apply to small places beyond the present objective which it might be advisable to take.

   If a batty should receive its orders too late to fire for the full 30 mins it should commence as soon as possible but it must only fire for the shortened period ending 30 minutes after zero. Fire during last 5 minutes to be intense.

15. Watches must be carefully set to Signal time & the times laid down for the lifts strictly adhered to.

16. In order that fire may be continued without interruption in case of a breakdown in the Signal Communications a programme and time table of the tasks allotted to each Battery will be kept at the Batty and in each O.P. allotted to the Battery. The programme and time table will not be taken forward beyond the O.P's.

Capt. R.F.A
Adj. 96 F.A Bde.

95th Bde Operation order N°1. cont.

Companies of 63rd Bde. & 1. Coy 62nd Bde.

to seize and consolidate the following:-

First Objective. Fricourt Farm - Trench Junction X.27.6.1½. Bouzefire Trench X.27.6.7e.4½. then advance 50.05 on the line Railway - copse. - south end of Shelter Wood.

Second objective X.29.6.5.6. (joining with 7th Divn) to X.23.6.65.65. where Quadrangle Trench crosses the Mametz-Contalmaison Rd. with advanced posts along Railway and Quadrangle ~~Trench~~ Support Trench.    During the advance to the second objective the N.E. end of Fricourt Wood will be seized and consolidated.

14.   Traffic Routes. ~~Pioneer Avenue~~ These are to be strictly adhered to:-

UP. Trench:  Pioneer Avenue & LIHIDUM AVENUE.
DOWN. Trenches.. KINGS AVENUE, QUEENS AVENUE
                         MIDDLESEX AVENUE.

As the advance continues one up and one down Trench will be constructed by the R.E's.

UP.    PIRFLEET  TO SUNKEN ROAD.
DOWN.  X.27.6.20. TO BALMORAL.

Picquets have been detailed off to turn out into the open any man using the trenches in the wrong direction.

15. Report Centres advanced Divl report centre at F.2.a½.27. In cases of emergency when reports dealing with the tactical situation cannot be transmitted to Bde HQrs this report centre will forward them by wire direct to Divl City H.Qrs. F.28.a.3½.

This method is only to be used as a last resort.

B. Welle. Capt R.A.
A.Adj 95th Bde

26-6.

## Smoke and Gas Barrage

### Smoke

1. A smoke barrage will be established from 7.20 a.m. to 7.50 a.m. on "Y" day. The following will therefore be substituted for the tasks mentioned for that period in Table "E". For tasks see "Smoke Barrage Table" and Sketch "S".

### Gas

2. A Gas Attack will be delivered along the front of the XV Corps during the night "V/W" provided the wind is suitable on night of "V/W".

3. If wind is not suitable, the attack will be made on night "W/X". If not suitable on that night, the attack will be made on night "X/Y". Corps HQ will issue orders by 6 pm whether the gas attack will take place on that particular day or not.

4. A heavy shrapnel barrage will be opened on the front line trenches. Trench Mortars will co-operate to the limit of their range. Communication Trenches will be searched by artillery and indirect machine gun fire. Reserve billets and communications will be heavily bombarded.

5. The tasks allotted in Table B.C.D etc will be cancelled for the period during which the gas attack is being made.

6. For tasks see attached "Gas Barrage Table" and Sketch "G".

7. Both the above tasks will be carried out by only one section per Battery.

8. The "Gas Barrage" will be carried out on receipt of message "CLARENCE BARRAGE at ........ (zero time)".

9. The "Smoke Barrage" will be carried out on receipt of message "BARRAGE CUTHBERT at ........ (zero time)".

B. Mellé Capt RFA.
Adj "96" Bde RFA

19-6-16.

A1

## Table "A" - Wirecutting "U" Day

| Battery | Time From | Time To | Task | Ammunition Shrapnel | Ammunition H.E. |
|---|---|---|---|---|---|
| A | 4 a.m. | 6.00 a.m. | Cut wire from X 27 d 0.4 to X 27 d 0.7 | About 300 Rds per gun | Nil |
|  | 9 a.m. | 11.00 a.m. | " X 27 c 6.2 to X 27 c 5.4 |  |  |
|  | 11.30 a.m. | 1.30 p.m. | " X 27 c 4.0.15 to X 27 c 15.40 |  |  |
|  | 4.30 a.m. | 6.30 p.m. | " X 25 c 15.50 to X 27 d 7.9 |  |  |
|  | 7.00 p.m. | 9.00 p.m. | " X 28 a 5.0 to X 28 a 3.2 |  |  |
| B | 6.30 a.m. | 8.30 a.m. | Cut wire from X 27 a 40.25 to X 27 c 2.4 | do | do |
|  | 9.00 a.m. | 11.00 a.m. | " X 27 c 15.40 to X 26 d 8.7 |  |  |
|  | 2.00 p.m. | 4.00 p.m. | " X 27 d 7.9 to X 27 d 30.95 |  |  |
|  | 4.30 p.m. | 6.30 p.m. | " X 28 a 3.2 to X 28 a 0.35 |  |  |
| C | 4.00 a.m. | 6.00 a.m. | Cut wire from X 27 d 0.7 to X 27 a 35.05 | do | do |
|  | 6.30 a.m. | 8.30 a.m. | " X 27 c 00.50 to X 27 c 0.7 |  |  |
|  | 11.30 a.m. | 1.30 p.m. | " X 27 c 4.6 to X 27 c 1.8 |  |  |
|  | 2.00 p.m. | 4.00 p.m. | " X 27 d 30.95 to X 27 d 0.9 |  |  |
|  | 7.00 p.m. | 9.00 p.m. | " X 28 a 0.35 to X 27 b 30.45 |  |  |

Wire Cut by 96th Bde.
— June 24-30" —

A 1*

Scale
1/10,000.

A —

## Table "B" Period 9.30 p.m. U to 9.30 a.m. V

| Battery | Task No | Time From | Time To | No of Guns | Task | Rounds per gun |
|---|---|---|---|---|---|---|
| C/96 | 47 | 9.30pm | 11.30pm | 2 | Search LOZENGE WOOD & SUNKEN ROAD on Sons, Berks & Fwoj Fwooj & Shrup... | 150 |
|  | 48 | 9.30pm | 10.30pm | 2 | Search Communication Trench WEST of SUNKEN ROAD | 30 |
|  | 49 | 10.30pm | 11.0pm | 1 | Sweep Trench & Trench RIGHT of RAILWAY COPSE 16 X 28 a 75 80 | 25 |
| A/96 | 52 | 3 am | 3.30am | 2 | Sweep CRUCIFIX TRENCH from PLOUGH 16 X 27 B. 94 | 50 |
|  | 53 | 3.30am | 4 am | 1 | Trench Tramway & Trench junc RAILWAY COPSE 16 X 28 a.75 80 | 25 |
|  | 54 | 4 am | 4.30am | 2 | Sweep CORN wood ... Trenches WEST of SUNKEN ROAD | 40 |
| B/96 | 50 | 11 pm | 12 mn | 2 | Sweep LOZENGE GULLY from PRUE TRENCH FARM 6 X 10 G 4 1 ? | 60 |
|  | 51 | 12 mn | 3 am | 2 | Front line bank Junction with ... GULLY SOUTH of ... | 50 |
|  | 59 | 7.30pm | 10am | 2 | Front line & SAP in EG 18 ab ... | 30 |
|  | 63 | 2.0pm | 2.30pm | ? | Sweep Communication Trench with ... Boyau & SAP ... | 80 |
| C/96 | 65 | 4 pm | 5.20pm | 4 | FRONT LINE & SHADY TRENCH | 72 |
|  | 69 | 7 pm | 8 pm | — | Sweep Track & Trench Tramway from Railway Copse 6 X 28 a.75 80 | 40 |
|  | 60 | 10 am | 11 am | — | Sweep LOZENGE ALLEY from PRUE POST FARM 6 X 10 G 4 0 | 80 |
| A/96 | 61 | 11 am | 12.30pm | — | Search POSITION Shelter SHELTER TRENCH mh.D. (64 & 65 & 4 from map squares) | 20 |
|  | 64 | 2.30pm | 4.0pm | — | Sweep CRUCIFIX Trench from Boyau h X 27 b.8 ... | 20 |
|  | 67 | 4 pm | 5.20pm | 4 | The PEAR & SOUTH Trench Junction X 28 a. ... | 8 |
|  | 70 | 8 pm | 9.30pm | — | Front line ... Apex of Triangle | 8 |
| B/96 | 56 | 4.30am | 5.30am | — | Sweep SUNKEN ROAD from X 27 D 2 a 45 to 12 CORN wood & Trench WEST of ... | 20 |
|  | 57 | 5.00am | 7 am | — | Sweep CRUCIFIX Trench & ... PROLONG h X 27 b. 9 4 | 30 |
|  | 58 | 7 am | 9.30am | — | Search LOZENGE WOOD | 30 |
|  | 62 | 12.30pm | 2 pm | — | Sweep SUNKEN ROAD & CORN & LOZENGE WOODS & Trench ... | 40 |
|  | 66 | 4 pm | 5.20pm | 4 | LOZENGE WOOD | 70 | S & H Shell |
|  | 68 | 5.20pm | 7 pm | — | Sweep LOZENGE WOOD & ALLEY from PRUE POST FARM 6 X 10 G 40 | 40 |

A₂  "Table B"  Period 9.30pm "U" to 9:30pm "Y"

| Bty | Task N° | Time From | Time To | Task | Ammunition H.E | Remarks |
|---|---|---|---|---|---|---|
| | 121 | 9.30pm | 9.30 | [illegible task] X27, G36, X27 G48, X27 G40 X27 K.20 X28 A 50 5  (Slow) | 240 | |
| | 122 | 5pm | 6.30pm | [illegible] X 26 + 4.10.75 X 21 & 20's (no remain unnecessary) | 120 | |
| | 123 | 6pm | 7pm | | 180 | |
| D196 (How) | 123 | 6.30pm | 9.30pm | LONGER LANE (no remain unnecessary) | | |
| | | 8pm | 9pm | | | |
| | | 9pm | | | | |
| | 124 | 9.30pm | 8.30pm | LOZENGE WOOD (30 rnds amm unnecessary) | 60 | |
| | | 4pm | 6pm | [illegible] X 27 G + 4 5 X 28 & 50's | 80 | |
| | 125 | 10.30pm | 3pm | [illegible] | 60 | |
| | 126 | 4pm | 5.30pm | | 60 | |

LOZENGE WOOD & SUNKEN ROAD to Nº 2 & 3
DUMMY & SUNKEN ROAD to Nº 4

"Table F"
Same as Table B

# TABLE "C"

## Period 9.30pm "V" to 9.30pm "W"

| BATTERY | TASK No | TIME FROM | TIME TO | TASK | AMMUNITION SHRAP | AMMUNITION H.E |
|---|---|---|---|---|---|---|
| A/96 | 47 | 9.30am | 4.30am | See Table "B" for sufficient Tasks | | 150 |
| | 67 | 11.30am | 2.30am | | | 80 |
| | 63 | 2.30am | 9am | | | 60 |
| | 65 | 9am | 10.20am | (Concentrated Bombardment 4am) | | 40 |
| | 69 | 10.20am | 11.30am | | | 40 |
| B/96 | 48 | 1am | 2am | | | 90 |
| | 49 | 3.30am | 4am | | | 20 |
| | 52 | 12.30am | 1am | | | 30 |
| | 53 | 2am | 2.30am | | | 25 |
| | 54 | 4am | 4.30am | | | 40 |
| | 60 | 4.30am | 6am | | | 100 |
| | 61 | 4am | 5.30am | | | 20 |
| | 64 | 2.30am | 4am | | | 80 |
| | 64 | 9am | 10.20am | (Concentrated Bombardment 4am) | | 40 |
| | 70 | 9pm | 9.30pm | | | 100 |
| C/96 | 50 | 2.30am | 3.30am | | | 50 |
| | 51 | 9.30am | 12.30am | " | 150 | |
| | 56 | 6am | 7am | | 20 | 20 |
| | 57 | 7.30am | 9am | | | 30 |
| | 58 | 4pm | 4.30pm | | | 30 |
| | 62 | 7am | 8.30am | | | 80 |
| | 66 | 9am | 10.20am | (Concentrated Bombardment 4am) | | 40 |
| | 68 | 3.30pm | 4pm | | | 80 |

A3

Tasks "C" Group 9:30am V.69??W

| BATTERY | TASK Nº | TIME FROM | TIME TO | TASK | H.E. | REMARKS |
|---|---|---|---|---|---|---|
|  | 121 | 8:30am | 9:30am | Y.S.R No.1 & Pa Table R | 240 |  |
|  | 130 | 9:30am | 9:30am | BOTTOM WOOD | 120 |  |
|  | 140 | 9:30am | 9am | LOZENGE — ALWET from x.17 Cond to x.17 C — 9 wilden | 90 |  |
| D/R6 | 126 | 9am | 10:40am | Pa R No.1&6 Pa Table B | 120 |  |
| (Pa) | 141 | 10:20am | 11:30am | CRUCIFIX | 20 |  |
|  | 143 | 11:30am | 1pm | PaR No.1&3 Pa Table B | 45 |  |
|  |  | 1pm | 4pm | PaR No.1&4  ·    B | 150 |  |
|  |  |  | 5pm | CRUCIFIX TRENCH x.17 b.7—to x.2. b.6.9 | 90 |  |

A4    Field "D" 0.30am W to 9.30pm X

| BATTERY | PARK | TIME | | TASK | ROUNDS | REMARKS |
| --- | --- | --- | --- | --- | --- | --- |
| | AT | FROM | TO | | | |
| D/96 (How) | 101 125 | 9.30pm 4.30am | 4.30am 8.30am | Task 121 Tar Tota. 78 Concentration Barrage | 200 80 | |
| | 126 130 | 6am 9am | 9am 12noon | Conc R 128 YoR 8 Conc R 132 " "B" | 80 120 | |
| | 131 135 140 | 12noon 3pm 4.30pm | 2pm 4pm 6pm | Conc R 139 YoR 143 " "C" YoR 145 " "C" | 80 120 | |
| | 145 150 | 6pm 6.30pm | 6.30pm 7pm | YoR 140 " "R" YoR 122 " "R" | 80 | |
| | | | | Counter bomb B. | | |
| | Yes | 7pm | 9pm | Yo R 142 Conc R 125 YoR B | 60 1 | |

# TABLE 'E'
## Period 9.30pm "X" to 9.30pm "Y"

| Battery | Task No | Time From | Time To | Task | Ammunition Shrap | Ammunition HE |
|---|---|---|---|---|---|---|
| A/96 | 48 | 9.30pm | 10.30pm | See Table B | | 70 |
| | 49 | 10.30pm | 11pm | " | | 25 |
| | 52 | 3 am | 3.30 am | " | | 50 |
| | 53 | 3.30 am | 4 am | " | | 25 |
| | 54 | 4 am | 4.30 am | " | | 40 |
| | 64 | 6 am | 7.20 am | Concentrated Bombardment | | 70 |
| | 60 | 10.30 am | 12 noon | See Table B | | 50 |
| | 61 | 12 noon | 1 pm | " | | 20 |
| | 67 | 4 pm | 5.20 pm | Concentrated Bombardment | | 30 |
| | 70 | 5.20 pm | 6 pm | See Table B | | 40 |
| | | 7 pm | 9 pm | Any points requiring special attention | | ? |
| B/96 | 51 | 12 midn | 3 am | See Table B | 150 | 30 |
| | 57 | 4.30 am | 6 am | " | | 70 |
| | 66 | 6 am | 7.20 am | Concentrated Bombardment | | 70 |
| | 62 | 7.30 am | 9.30 am | See Table B | | 40 |
| | 56 | 1 pm | 3 pm | " | 20 | 20 |
| | 58 | 3 pm | 4 pm | " | | 30 |
| | 62 | 4 pm | 5.20 pm | Concentrated Bombardment | | 30 |
| | 66 | 5.30 pm | 6 pm | See Table B | | 40 |
| | 68 | 6 pm | 7 pm | " | | 40 |
| | | 7 pm | 9 pm | Any points requiring special attention | | ? |
| | 50 | 11 pm | 12 mid | See Table B | | 60 |
| C/96 | 47 | 9.30 pm | 4.30 am | " | | 140 |
| | 65 | 6 am | 7.20 am | Concentrated Bombardment | | 70 |
| | 63 | 9.30 am | 10.30 am | See Table B | | 30 |
| | 59 | 4 pm | 5.20 pm | Concentrated Bombardment | | 30 |
| | | 7 pm | 9 pm | Any points requiring special attention | | ? |

A 5

July 5: 0.30 pm "X" to 9.30 pm "Y"

| Battery | Task No | Time From | Time To | TASK | Ammunition Remaining |
|---|---|---|---|---|---|
| D/96 (Tom) | 121 | 1.30 pm | 4.30 pm | H on Table B | 200 |
| | 122 | 4.30 pm | 6 am | YaR 22 Table B 30 rounds on each concn | 60 |
| | 126 | 10.30 am | 12 noon | Continuation Sukarno | 120 |
| | 144 | 6 am | 7.20 am | YaR 126 Table B | 60 |
| | | 7.30 am | 10.30 am | YaR 124 20 rounds on each concn | 40 |
| | 123 | 12 noon | 2 pm | YaR 128 Table B | 30 |
| | 126 | 2 am | 3 am | 125 B | 30 |
| | | 3 am | 4 pm | | 60 |
| | 142 | 4.30 pm | 5.20 pm | Quiet of L1 Bombardment YaR 142 12.0? | 60 |
| | 139 | 5.20 pm | 6 pm | YaR 139 "DLT" | 60 |
| | 120 | 6 pm | 6.30 pm | 140 "C" | 40 |

TABLE "H" - 96th BRIGADE R.F.A.

| TIME FROM | TIME TO | NO. OF GUNS TO BE EMPLOYED | LIMITS OF TASK | ROUNDS PER GUN SHRAP. | ROUNDS PER GUN H.E. | REMARKS |
|---|---|---|---|---|---|---|
| -0.65 | -0.30 | 8 A+B | Front & Support Trenches from X.27.c.4.2.to X.26.d.8065 | 7 | 11 | Section Fire 1 minute |
| -0.30 | -0.10 | 8 A+B | Do X.27.central to X.27.b.2095 | 8 | 12 | Section Fire 30 seconds |
| -0.10 | 0.0 | 8 A+B | Do | 8 | 12 | Section Fire 15 seconds |
| -0.65 | -0.10 | 4 C | Do X.27.central to X.27.b.2095 | 4 | 20 | Bursts of fire at about 5 minutes interval. |
| -0.10 | 0.0 | 4 C | Do | 4 | 16 | Section Fire 15 seconds |
| 0.4 | 0.17 | 8 A+B | X.27.d.0540 to X.27.b.0.1. | 9 | 4 | Section Fire 30 seconds |
| 0.4 | 0.17 | 4 C | X.28.b.2500 to X.28.c.60.60. | 5 | 8 | Section Fire 30 seconds |
| 0.19 | 0.45 | 8 A+B | X.28.c.2.9. to X.27.b.9035 | 17 | 9 | Section Fire 30 seconds |
| 0.17 | 0.45 | 2 C | X.23.c.9.1. to X.23.c.7.5. | 2 | 12 | Section Fire 1 minute |
| 0.17 | 0.45 | 2 C | area round X.24.a.2.4. | 2 | 12 | Section Fire 1 minute |
| 0.46 | 1.15 | 8 A+B | X.28.b.2.1. to X.28.a.6.6. | 20 | 9 | Section Fire 30 seconds |
| 0.45 | 1.15 | 2 C | X.29.a.0.8. to X.22.d.0.2. | 15 | 15 | Section Fire 30 seconds |
| 0.45 | 1.15 | 2 C | X.29.b.4098 to X.23.c.8.5. |  | 30 | Section Fire 30 seconds |
| 1.15 | 2.25 | 8 A+B | X.28.b.2.1. to X.28.a.9575 | 30 | 10 | Bursts of fire |
| 1.15 | 2.25 | 4 C | X.29.b.4096 to X.23.c.8.5. | 5 | 15 | Bursts of fire |
| 2.33 | 2.55 | 8 A+B | X.30.a.1.8. to X.24.c.3545 | 16 | 6 | Section Fire 30 seconds |
| 2.55 | - | 8 A+B | X.30.a.1.7. to X.24.c.1.6. | 12 | 8 | Section Fire 30 seconds |

BM/007/2

A6.   Aeroplane photograph shows new trench running from X.28.d.9.8. through BOTTOM WOOD (25 yards east of Western edge of Wood) to QUADRANGLE TRENCH at X.23.c.4.6.  The tasks of Howitzer Batteries of 95th and 96th Brigades in Table "H" are therefore altered.

The following will be substituted for Table "H" (4.5 Howitzers) previously issued.

| UNIT | TIME FROM | TIME TO | NO. OF GUNS | TASK | AMMUNITION |
|---|---|---|---|---|---|
| 96th Brigade 4.5 Howitzers | -0.65 | -0.10 | 4 | X.27.c.4.8. to X.27.a.3.4. and LOZENGE ALLEY | 20 |
| | -0.10 | 0.0 | 4 | Do              Do | 12 |
| | 0.0 | 0.17 | 4 | X.27.b.6.6. to X.21.d.5025 | 12 |
| | 0.17 | 0.45 | 4 | X.23.a.5015 & CRUCIFIX TRENCH | 10 |
| | 0.45 | 1.15 | 2 | X.28.b.9.9. to X.22.d.0.2. | 20 |
| | 0.45 | 1.15 | 2 | Trench Front edge of BOTTOM WOOD | 25 |
| | 1.15 | 2.30 | 4 | Trench from X.28.d.6.4. to X.29.a.0500 (l.0.8) (New Trench) | 40 |
| | 2.30 | 2.55 | 4 | X.23.d.3555 to X.23.b.3.2. | 18 |
| | 2.55 | further orders. | 2 | X.24.c.1.6. to X.23.d.5.6. | |

## TABLE I

| | | TIME | | TASK | | |
|---|---|---|---|---|---|---|
| | | FROM | TO | | | |
| A/76 | 47 | 9:30am | 10:30am | | | /30 |
| | 6 | 7:30am | 12am | | | 80 |
| | 48 | | 2:30am | | | 80 |
| | 80 | | 0.2am | | | 70 |
| | | 7am | 9pm | | | 47 |
| B/76 | 57 | 9:30am | 10:30am | | | 80 |
| | | 10:30am | 11am | | | 25 |
| | | 3am | 3:30am | | | 50 |
| | 63 | 9:30am | 4am | | | 25 |
| | 91 | 4am | 4:30am | | | 40 |
| | 50 | 10am | 11am | | | 80 |
| | 6 | 1am | 2:30am | | | 80 |
| | 54 | 2:30am | 4pm | | | 90 |
| | | 4pm | 6:30pm | Concentrated Dailand | | 90 |
| | 70 | 6am | 9:30pm | | | 100 |
| 3/76 | 50 | 7pm | 12midn | | | 30 |
| | | | 3am | | | |
| | 90 | 4:30am | 5:30am | | | 40 |
| | 67 | 5:30am | 7am | | | 30 |
| | 65 | 7am | 1:30am | | | 30 |
| | 63 | 2:30pm | 4pm | | | 40 |
| | 66 | 4pm | 5:30pm | Completed Saturation | | 70 |
| | 68 | 5:30pm | 7pm | | | 40 |

| TIME | | Battery | TASK | Ammunition | | REMARKS |
|---|---|---|---|---|---|---|
| FROM | TO | | | No. of Rounds | No. | |
| AM 7.20 | AM 7.21 | A | Enemy Party emerged X.24.c.05.70 X.19.c.90.10 | 16 | 16 | |
| | | B | X.19.b.85.40 X.24.a.00.85 | 16 | | |
| | | C | Enemy troops reported X.24.b.65.9 X.24.a.95.95 | 16 | | |
| | | D | X.24.b.10.20 | | 10 | |
| 7.21 | 7.28 | A | Report from X.24.c.66.15 X.24.c.70.30.55 | 16 | | |
| | | B | X.24.c.35.55 to X.26.a.0.65 | 10 | | |
| | | C | X.19.d.a.60 X.19.c.85.95 | 10 | 10 | |
| | | D | | | | |
| 7.28 | 7.36 | A | | | | |
| | | B | Enemy observed in sunken road X.19.b.4.7 | 8 | 8 | |
| | | C | | | | |
| | | D | | | | |
| 7.36 | 7.37 | A | ditto | 1 | 1 | |
| | | B | | | | |
| | | C | | | | |
| 7.37 | 7.39 | A | Enemy Group seen from X.26.b.5.4 | 0000 | 0 | |
| | | B | | | | |
| | | C | | | | |

21st Divisional Artillery.

------------

96th BRIGADE R. F. A.

AUGUST 1916.

Army Form C. 2118.

# WAR DIARY
## or
## INTELLIGENCE SUMMARY.

(Erase heading not required.)

Sheet 48

Instructions regarding War Diaries and Intelligence Summaries are contained in F. S. Regs., Part II. and the Staff Manual respectively. Title pages will be prepared in manuscript.

| Place | Date | Hour | Summary of Events and Information | Remarks and references to Appendices |
|---|---|---|---|---|
| | 24th 25th 26th 27th July | | The Brigade moved from FRICOURT to ARRAS and BONNAY - BETHENCOURT - NEUF MOULIN - FROHEN LE PETIT - BERLENCOURT - WANQUETIN. | |
| | 31st July 3rd Aug | | The guns were overhauled at HABARCQ | |
| | 4th " | | Took over from 48th Bde R.F.A. XIV Div (Lt Col Browne C.M.G. R.F.A) Reinforced F. Sector extending from G.36.c.27 to the river SCARPE (Ref 1/20,000 51 NW 3) A section of B/97 was placed under B[de] Comdr for Tactical purposes. The Brigade was disposed as follows:— | |

| | Battery Position | Section B/97 | Post w/c | O P | | |
|---|---|---|---|---|---|---|
| A/96 | | | G.20.d.53 | G.29.B.05.75 | G.30.B.27 | The SCARPE |
| B/96 | | | G.20.d.59 | G.29.B.17 | CAMBRAI Road | G.30.B.27 |
| C/96 | | | G.26.c.6[?] | G.29.c.64 | G.36.c.27 | CAMBRAI Road The SCARPE |
| D/96 | | | G.27.c.77 | G.29.d.27 | G.36.c.27 | WAGON LINES (just) Between WANQUETIN |

**Army Form C. 2118.**

# WAR DIARY
## or
## INTELLIGENCE SUMMARY.
(Erase heading not required.)

Sheet 49.

| Place | Date | Hour | Summary of Events and Information | Remarks and references to Appendices |
|---|---|---|---|---|
| | Aug 18-19 | | I. Section was reinforced. A/95 (Capt Lee M.C.) and C/97 (Capt Dalton) were placed under the orders of the Bde Comdr and the section B/97 rejoined its Battery | |
| | 19-20 | | Battery line dispersed as follows: | |

Battery | Position | O.C. | Ground Covered
--- | --- | --- | ---
A/96 | | No change | 
A/97 | G.20.d. 55.05 | | G.30.I.27 — Railway / Ruin SCARPE
B/96 | No change | | No change
C/97 | G.26.D.30.15 | | 100ʸ N+S of CAMBRAI road
C/96 | No change | | No change
D/96 | No change | | No change

| | 26. | | C/96 was shelled by a 4.2" howitzer about 40 rounds being fired. A gun emplacement was hit but however no damage was done. | |
| | 29. | | The Brigade was reorganised into two 6 gun 18p Batteries and on 4.5"+4gun Battery "A" Batty was split up, its Right Section and HQ going to C/96 (Major T M Brown) and Left Section to B/96 (Capt Parker M.C.) A/97 which had now become A/95 and a section of C/97 now C/94 was placed under 8th Canadian F. Brigade. 96 Bde Group ... They were now disposed as follows | |

Army Form C. 2118.

# WAR DIARY
## or
## INTELLIGENCE SUMMARY.
(Erase heading not required.)

Sheet 50

| Place | Date | Hour | Summary of Events and Information | Remarks and references to Appendices |
|---|---|---|---|---|

Battery | | | O.P. | Ground covered from

B/96 | | | 4 guns No change | No change | CAMBRAI Rd | G.30.b.27
      |     |     | 2 guns G.20.d.5.3 | | |

C/96 | | | 4 guns No change | | G.36.c.27 | CAMBRAI Rd
     |    |    | 2 guns G.26.B.30.15 | | |

Section C/96 | | | G.26.B.30.15 | | |

A/95 | | | 4 guns G.20.a.55.05 | G.29.B | G.30.B.27 | River SCARPE
     |    |   | 2 guns G.20.d.5.3  | 35.75 | |

D/96 | | | No change | No change | | No change

COURSES 2/Lt Williamson & Sgt Nathan B/96 to VI" Corps. Army School (FOSSEUX Chateau)
2 N.C.O's (C & D) to same school
1 officer (C/96) to Divn Anti-Gas school (HAUTEVILLE)
1 Sgt to 12 Squadron R.F.C. Winters Corner

WORK DONE Forward positions for 6 gun batty begun by B/96 & C/96 in G.28 central
Wagon Lines WANQUETIN were begun to be prepared & to water Horse Nosebags & Shelter
Being made.

#353  Wt. W2544/1454  700,000  3/15  D.D.& L.  A.D.S.S./Forms/C. 2118.

# WAR DIARY
## or
## INTELLIGENCE SUMMARY.

Army Form C. 2118.

Sheet 51

| Place | Date | Hour | Summary of Events and Information | Remarks and references to Appendices |
|---|---|---|---|---|
| A Woods | | | Capn N. M. McLEOD D/96. Military Cross | |
| | | | 35451. Cpl. HODGKISS H.Q. Military Medal | |
| | | | 82928 Gnr DIGGLE " do | |
| | | | 82645 Dr LEE " do | |
| | | | 83978 Gnr SPENCER D/96 do | |
| | | | No important operations took place in I Section during the month the enemy being limited against working parties etc. | |
| | 2/9/16 | | | |

J. McGowan RMA
Major RFA
Comdg 96"B" RFA

21st Divisional Artillery.

96th BRIGADE R.F.A.

SEPTEMBER 1916.

2/9th Div.

96th Brigade
Sheet 52. RFA V.M.13

Army Form C. 2118.

# WAR DIARY
## or
## INTELLIGENCE SUMMARY.
(Erase heading not required.)

| Place | Date | Hour | Summary of Events and Information | Remarks and references to Appendices |
|---|---|---|---|---|
| | 1-9-16 | | Very quiet in the evening of the 3rd C Battery avoided our right in a small Rd | |
| | 2-9-16 | | Relieved by 157" B.de R.F.A. 35" Division on the night 9/10 & 10/11 | |
| | 9-6-15 | | Arrived BERTENCOURT and went into billets | |
| | 11" | | SARTON | |
| | 12" | | " | |
| | 13" | | " BELLEVUE Fme. (ALBERT). Batteries went into action near BAZENTIN LE GRAND. | |
| | | | WOOD. B/96 was attached to 94th Group (Col Barnish) C/96 to 95th Group (Col Fitzgerald) and D/96 (Hew) to Corps Artillery for counter Battery work. Brigade H.Q. remained in new POMIERES REDOUBT. the Batteries remaining tactically in the above Wagon lines during the month. The usual musketry administration was carried on by 96 Bde. D/96 was afterwards attached to 35 Group for tactical purposes. Col Bowring was away commanding 183 Bde RFA. | |
| | 22-10-16 1st Oct | | Awards during month '470 13 Cpl Shepherd E. D/96. Military Medal | |
| | | | Casualties: Officers Killed. Capt. G L Johnstone C/96 | |
| | | | Wounded. Maj TM Clements DSO 2/Lt J R Graham C/96. 2/Lt ST Holbourne C/96. | |
| | | | | Bruere Cap: |
| | | | O/R Ranks Killed - 9. | |
| | | | Wounded - 27. | 15·10·16 |
| | | | | O.C. 96 B.de R.F.A |

21st Divisional Artillery.

96th BRIGADE R. F. A.

OCTOBER 1916.

**Army Form C. 2118.**

96th Brigade RFA Vol 14
Sheet 53.

# WAR DIARY
## or
## INTELLIGENCE SUMMARY.
*(Erase heading not required.)*

| Place | Date | Hour | Summary of Events and Information | Remarks and references to Appendices |
|---|---|---|---|---|
| SOMME. | 12th - 13th | | Batteries in action under 96th and 94th Bde Groups on in September. | A |
| " | 13/14th 14/15th | | Batteries were relieved by Batteries of the 12th Div Art. | |
| | 14th | 9am | Sections relieved on the night 13/14th marched to La Neuville via FRICOURT - MEAULTE - HEILLY - BONNAY. Arrived 3pm. | |
| | 15th | " | " " " 14/15th " " " " " " Arrived | |
| | | 2pm | Men in good billets. | |
| | 16th | 9am | Bde. marched to VILLERS-BOCAGE via QUERRIEU - RAINNEVILLE. Arrived 12.30pm. Men in billets | |
| | 17th | 7.30am | " " AUTHIEULE via LA VICOGNE - BEAUVAL - DOULLENS. Arrived 12.15pm. Officers & men in huts. | |
| | 18th | 9am | " " AUBROMETZ via HAMBERCOURT - BRETEL - HEM - BAILY - BONNIERS. Arrived 2.30pm. Men in billets | |
| | | 11.30am | Advanced Party of one Officer + 2 men per Battery + HQrs proceeded by Bus to SAILLY LA BOURSE to 5th Bde RHA. 8th Division. | |
| | 19th | 8am | Bde. marched to FONTAINE LEZ DOULANS via FILLIEVRES - LINZEUX - OEUF - BEAUVOIS - PIERREMONT - AN VIN. Arrived 2.30pm. Men in billets | |
| | 20th | 9am | " " LA PUGNOY via NEUCHIN - PERNES. Arrived 1.45pm. Men in billets. Throughout this march from the SOMME the work of the billeting parties was much facilitated by the Town Major, who had everything ready beforehand - a great improvement, as we formerly worked with the Mayor and were often were deprived of the best places. | |
| | 21st | 7.30am | Bde. & Bty Commanders proceeded by Bus up to the new Battery Positions. Returned about 7/pm | |
| | | 9am | One Section per Bty marched to Wagon Lines of 5th Bde Batteries and guns were taken up same night. | |
| | 22nd | 9am | Remaining Sections moved up and relief of 5th Bde RHA completed. 533rd How Bty (Major G.W. Haynes RFA TF) was absorbed into the Brigade and renamed H Battery 96 Bde RFA. This Battery had only left England on the 7th inst. and had been in action for about a week. | |

Army Form C. 2118.

# WAR DIARY
## or
## INTELLIGENCE SUMMARY.
*(Erase heading not required.)*

Sheet 54

| Place | Date | Hour | Summary of Events and Information | Remarks and references to Appendices |
|---|---|---|---|---|
| ANNEQUIN | 22. | | Gun Positions, OP's & Magazines were disposed as follows shown in | B |
| | 23/6 31st | | Guns were examined by I.O.M. No. 1 Ordnance Workshops. BETHUNE and a few minor repairs were carried out during the next few days at the Workshops. | |
| | | | Batteries were busy calibrating and registering. Bate Section was known as CAMBRIN SECTOR. Enemy gun fire practically nil. | |
| | | | " T.M. " very troublesome at times but were effectively stopped by concentrated bursts of fire from 18 Pdrs, 4.5" Hows. T.Mortars attacks Artillery for about 10 minutes on the suspected mortar. A Battery assisted 5" How. Out on our left to knock out some mortars at the junction of W.O. Section. Operation lasted about 3 days, hundreds of fire being employed about twice a day. Aeroplane reported trenches well damaged by fire of A/96. | |
| | | | During the month the following awards were given :- | |
| | | | Military Cross : 2/Lt. J.R. Graham C/96. (since died of wounds) | |
| | | | D.C.M. : BSM Freeman D/96. | |
| | | | Following NCO's & men proceeded to England to join a Cadet School | |
| | | | Sgt Dunstan C/96. | |
| | | | Bdr Ayres B/96 | |
| | | | Gr Cook HQrs/96. | |
| | | | Following attended 1st Army T.M. School : 2/Lt Hutchinson D/96 & 6 men. | |
| | 31-10-16. | | | |

M Fanthey Lieut. Col. RHA.
Comdg. 96th Bde RFA.

"A"

## 21ST DIVISIONAL ARTILLERY.
### INSTRUCTIONS FOR RELIEF NO.1.

Reference XV Corps C.A.10/310 dated 11th forwarded to you yesterday:-

1. 94th Bde Group will be relieved by 62nd Brigade Group.

    A/62 will relieve A/94
    B/62   :    :    B/94
    C/62   :    :    C/94
    D/62   :    :    D/94
    A/64   :    :    B/96

    O.C. 94th Brigade Group will arrange to send guides to S.23.a.1.7. (present HQrs of 62nd Bde R.F.A.) to meet one officer per Battery and to guide them to the units they will relieve. Guides to be at S.23.a.1.7. at 11.am. tomorrow 13th instant.

    62nd Brigade Group will not take over the Wagon Lines of 94th Brigade Group, but will remain in their present wagon lines.

2. 95th Brigade will be relieved by a Brigade of 29th Divnl. Artillery. Batteries will be relieved by opposite numbers.

    C/95 will be relieved by B/84.
    D/95  :    :    :    :  a Howr Bty of 29th Div.Art.
    Brigade and Battery Commanders and a proportion of telephon-ists of 29th D.A. Bde will arrive at 95th Bde HQrs tomorrow. Time of arrival will be notified later.

    O.C. 95th Brigade Group will send a guide to S.23.a.1.7. tomorrow 13th instant at 11.am. to meet an officer of B/84 and to guide him to battery position of C/95.

3. In all cases, one section will be relieved on night 13/14th and remainder on night 14/15th.

4. 21st D.A.C. will be relieved by 12th D.A.C. Further instructions will be issued by Staff Captain.

5. Brigade and Battery Commanders of 21st Divisional Artillery will remain in command of their respective units until the relief is complete.

6. Brigade Commanders will arrange all details of times of relief, necessary guides, etc, with their opposite numbers.

7. All stores likely to be of any assistance to incoming units will be handed over (see para.5. of Corps Artillery letter).

S.C. 6/3

In continuation of this office, "Instructions for Relief" issued to-day:-

1. With reference to paras: 1 and 2:-
Ammunition will be handed over by Groups, - 94th. Brigade being responsible for the ammunition of "B"/96th. and 95th. Brigade for that of "C"/96th. and "D".
Great care will be taken that all ammunition is handed over, and receipts obtained.
All ammunition whether in present, or vacated positions must be handed over, including any ammunition that may still remain in the positions vacated by 14th. Divisional Artillery.

2. With reference to para: 4:-
The ammunition dump at S.9.d.5.0. will be taken over by the 12th. D.A.C. at 12 Noon on 14th. instant, at which hour the party from 21st. D.A.C. now at the dump, will be removed.
The 12th. D.A.C. will not take over the camp of the 21st. D.A.C. at POMMIERS REDOUBT.

3. With reference to para: 7:-
All tents and tarpaulins handed over to Units of 21st. Divisional Artillery by 14th. Divisional Artillery must be handed over to 12th. Divisional Artillery, and receipts obtained.

4. With reference to para: 10:-
The Trench Mortar Brigade will not move from their present camp until the morning of the 15th. instant. Arrangements for transport and destination will be notified later.

5. With reference to para: 12:-
The sections which are relieved on the night 13/14th. will march to the new billeting area on the morning of the 14th. instant. Time of starting, route, and destination will be notified later.

6. Billeting parties will meet the Staff-Captain in the new area on the morning of the 14th. at a time and place to be notified later.

7. Instructions as to supplies will be issued later.

8. Statements of amounts of ammunition handed over by 94th.& 95th. Brigade Groups, and at the Dump will be sent to this office as soon as possible after completion of the relief.

Captain, R.A.
12th. Oct: 1916. Staff-Captain, 21st. Divisional Artillery.

DISTRIBUTION.

94th. Bde RFA.      6
95th.  -do-         6
96th.  -do-         2
Trench Mortar Bde   4
21st. D.A.C.        6

## "B"

Gun Positions, O.Ps. & Wagon Lines of 36th Bde R.F.A. (CAMBRIN GROUP)

Reference 1/20,000 36c N.W.

| Unit | Battery Position | O.P. | Wagon Lines | Zone Covered. Boyaux. | Remarks |
|---|---|---|---|---|---|
| HQrs | F.23.d.8.9. |  | E.18.b.6.2. |  |  |
| A | F.30.c.2.4. | "Four Hundred" A.20.d.9.6. | F.14.d.5.8. | 5 10 27. |  |
| B | F.30.a.9.6. | "Tower of Babel" A.20.d.9.7. | L.2.c.8.3. | 5 10 16. |  |
| C | F.30.a.8.8. (4 guns) F.14.c.9.8.✕ (Enfilade Section) | "The Babe" A.20.d.75.48. | F.7.a.8.9. | 16 10 27. | ✕ One gun enfilades Close Support Trench in A.28.a. One gun enfilades Support Trench of Hohenzollern Sector, the Infantry of this Sector having a call on this gun. |
| D | G.1.b.4.7. | "Four Hundred" A.20.d.9.6. | F.14.d.5.8. | 5 10 27. |  |

31.10.16.

B Melle    Capt. R.F.A.
Adjutant, 90th Bde. R.F.A.

21st Divisional Artillery.
------------

96th BRIGADE R. F. Q. ::: NOVEMBER 1916.

# WAR DIARY
## INTELLIGENCE SUMMARY

| Date | Hour | Summary of Events and Information | Remarks |
|---|---|---|---|
| | | Capt N R G Shepherd D.H.<br>Robin Hunter G. D.H.<br>56439 Gnr Langton J.A. 11/9/16 Previous Injuries<br>55450 Gnr " E. 11/9/16 do<br>47015 Gnr Shepherd E. D/96. do<br>82325 " Doyle G. 11/9/16 do<br>56168 Br Jay F. 11/9/16 | |
| | | The following were wounded Previously Reported as the 11th Corps Commander:—<br>56465 Sgt Haynes A. C/96<br>46730 " Cook S.H. D/96<br>36430 Bm Young S.P. B/96<br>The following Officers wounded are now the month | |
| | | The following Casualties occurred —<br>10 r(Acting B.C.) Shand ? 91? to Major R.F.A. ??/1/16 ??/A Mountain Bty.<br>Lt. A Grey signed (Col.) — 1 / R Bain 13/9/16.<br>?? Orders w.e.f. 1 Sept 1916.<br>Capt? ?? ?? Following Instant ?? ?? Col ??<br>wef 14 Septer ?? confirmed in Rank.<br>BHQ { Lieut S J Dew to Major<br>T/Lieut K Grantley to Captain | |
| 20/1/16 | | | |

G W Taylor Major R.F.A.<br>Commanding 96th Brigade R.F.A.

21st Divisional Artillery.

## 96th BRIGADE R. F. A.

### DECEMBER 1916.

# WAR DIARY or INTELLIGENCE SUMMARY

Army Form C. 2118.

96 Bde R.F.A. Vol 16

Sheet 58.

| Place | Date | Hour | Summary of Events and Information | Remarks and references to Appendices |
|---|---|---|---|---|
| ANNEQUIN | 7.12.16 | — | 38th Bde R.F.A. relieved the 96th Bde as follows:- two infilade section. | |
| | 8.12.16 | | C/58 relieved A/96: 24th Batty relieved B/96: 72nd Batty relieved C/96: A/96 relieved D/96. Head Quarters B.C. & D/96 moved into rest at NOEUX-LES-MINES. | |
| | 11.12.16 | — | The enfilade section of C/96 & also A/96 came under the orders of the HOHENZOLLERN GROUP for tactical purposes. The TRAMWAY SCHEME was finally closed by a concentrated fire on point "A". This was carried out by the 158th Bde R.F.A. who had relieved the 96th Bde. | |
| NOYELLES | 12.12.16 | — | LT. COL. COURTNEY relieved Head Quarters 96th Bde R.F.A. near Tactical Command of the HOHENZOLLERN GROUP from LT. COL. FITZGERALD & 95th Bde Head Quarters. | |
| | 15.12.16 | — | 64th Inf. Bde relieved 110th Inf. Bde in the HOHENZOLLERN SECTOR | |
| | 16.12.16 | — | Bombardment of enemy's salient at G.12.d.5.8. in which A/96 participated | |
| | 20.12.16 | — | Bombardment of enemy's defences from H.7.c.0.3 to G.12.d.90.67 in which A/96 shelled Tunnel junction at H.7.c.15.62. | |
| | 23.12.16 | — | Enemy's artillery was much more active during the morning & in retaliation we carried out following bombardments viz | |
| | | 1.30 p.m. | Tunnel junction G.12.b.95.70. | |
| | | 2.5 p.m. | Trenches G.4.b.6.6 to G.4.b.73.63. | |
| | | 3.15 p.m. | Tunnel junction G.12.a.25.85. | |
| | 24.12.16 | — | About 10.30 a.m. the enemy started shelling 96th Bde Head Quarters was on lines at L.10.d.1.8 with size 5.9's killing one man (Gr DAUBENY) & wounding one horse. The lines were shifted to NOEUX-LES-MINES the following day. | |

# WAR DIARY
## or
## INTELLIGENCE SUMMARY

*(Erase heading not required.)*

Army Form C. 2118.

| Place | Date | Hour | Summary of Events and Information | Remarks and references to Appendices |
|---|---|---|---|---|
| NOYELLES | 24.12.16 | — | Sheet 59. Xmas shoot as per Battalion programme was carried out. As well as noticing not only annoyed the enemy very considerably but also practised the batteries in all the various schemes that had been evolved from time to time. | (?) |
| | 28.12.16 | — | 15th Infantry Bde relieved the 64th Infantry Bde in the HOHENZOLLERN SECTOR during the period 8.12.16 to 31.12.16. B.C. D/95 Bde briefside relieved 3/95 Bde in centre at NOEUX-LES-MINES. | (?) |
| | 29.12.16 | | From 10pm 27th to 4am 28th the enemy fired about 10,000 gas shells as general on battery positions around CAMBRIN + ANNEQUIN but did little or no damage except to the shelling & its shelling on the 23rd very little hostile artillery fire took place during the month, the infantry being only wounded by Trench Mortars which were generally very quickly silenced by the 4.5 hows. Adverse weather prevented the R.F.C from registering more than 3 or 4 targets. CAPT. PARK + CAPT. McLEOD were granted special leave for one month. Following officers attended courses during the month. LT. TIMSON - B.C's COURSE at SHOEBURYNESS + LARK HILL. LT. KING + LT. BEE - GAS Course at SAILLY - LA BOURSE. LT. PIERCE - GUNNERY Course at AIRE. LT. BARCLAY - TRENCH MORTAR Course at CLARQUES. | |

31.12.16.

H.H.Humphreys Lt/Col R.F.A
Cmdg 95th A de R.F.A.

www.ingramcontent.com/pod-product-compliance
Lightning Source LLC
Chambersburg PA
CBHW081542160426

43191CB00011B/1818